K R O H

The Greening of a Small Planet

and

C R O C

*Love and Power Politics
in Swamptown, YO*

by

Nina Galen

Copyright © 1999 by Nina Galen

Library of Congress Catalog Card Number: 99-97245
ISBN 1-58500-595-9

ABOUT THIS BOOK

CROC – Love and Power Politics in Swamptown, YO, a political satire, is the story of two deeply-in-love, star-crossed crocodiles who run for the same U.S. Senate seat on opposite tickets. Crocadolly, a Demodile, runs on an ecology platform. Young Rockadial, innocent stooge of greedy old Crockafeller, runs against big government and Federal taxation, as a Repelican.

Not for the faint of heart, this extremely funny yarn can turn deadly and tragic as suddenly as a crocodile striking its prey

KROH – The Greening of a Small Planet   This satire on the global economy concerns a diverse group of nineteen Earthlings (including an Economist, a Navajo, two Politicians, a Rabbi, a Psychiatrist, a Duck, and two Crocodiles) that travels to the planet Kroh to see if it is ripe for trade with Earth.

Some in the Delegation bring along schemes that will help them profit personally, without regard for the planet's inhabitants and ecology. Others are on quests of self-discovery. The Krohtians, teddy-bearish creatures with the minds of men, are happy to see the visitors come, and glad to see them go.

All author's royalties will go to protect and increase wildlife habitats.

Crocodile drawing by David Levine.

CROC

*Love and Power Politics
in Swamptown, YO*

CONTENTS

CROCAMAMA

Tranquility reigned in Swamptown, YO,
population 2 0 9.
Crocamama waited on a long, wavy line
to pay her water tax,
clasping a handbag fabricated from
the well-tanned hide
of that Yorkshire terrier
who never denied he'd found it scarier
trying to swim
with four big teeth sunk into him
than not; his supple, hirsute skin
now filled with gold doubloons,
former legal tender in some
tough, perhaps illegal double dealings of
long-dead Spanish merchants;
coin recently sucked
from the rank crustacean muck
of a sunken wreck by Martin Searles,
the charming treasure-seeker,
whose million-dollar hunch
resulted in (*Oh, God! No!*)
quite a sodden bunch
of pockets stuffed with coin
and misdirected crabs
(and aren't those pearls that were his eyes?)
she'd joined that day for lunch.

And feeling just fine, Crocamama was,
now that Rockadial,
her lazy, accident-prone son,
struck last Friday by a two-ton truck
on Interstate 9 5
and nearly road-killed (still alive,
but six days in a coma);
maybe now, the Lord be praised,
he'd change his wicked ways

and act more like he oughter:
stop jay-walking, scaring tourists off,
and wasting water.

ROCKADIAL

When young Rockadial
awakened from his coma
and found himself surrounded
by ecologists, folk who shyly,
then with greater zeal,
squeeze-dried his tail,
admired his sutures,
offered him a chance
at seven different eco-futures
(three archival, four in native dance).
He, while saying nothing,
personally preferred
consorting with a certain alligator bird,
lying in the sun with her on top,
pecking parasites and tickling his hide.

Yes, when Rockadial awoke
from his long coma,
realized he had nearly died,
quickly checked out his persona
and found it – Praise the Lord! –
still stuffed with soul,
his first words were:
Let the good times roll.

CROCKAFELLER

Crockafeller, sitting on his hillock,
studied his reflection in his private pool,
drew back his lips, wrinkled up his snout,
and seeing he was getting
longer in the tooth, stuck his tongue out
at his wrinkled image.

Ha! Only yesterday
had he been challenged to
a pecking-order scrimmage
by some macho whipper snapper.
No problemo!
He was still top croc
and would remain so.
Boss of Swamptown and all southern YO,
he'd sent that poor swain
packing. For, you see,
a croc as top as he
had no need *himself* to tussle,
could instead call in some hired muscle,
as Crockafeller always did
when needing to protect his hustle.

But on this date
more urgent business filled his plate.
Like whom to hire –
which charismatic, brain-dead crocoliar –
as congressional-committee
expert witness, to fulminate against
each piece of pro-environmental legislation
that might endanger
all the perfectly regressive
tolls, taxations, and assessments

that he personally levied
on inhabitants of every
marsh and morass,
bog, ditch, dike, and shoal
within his purview and control?

Who send to Washington
to advocate his cause?
His eye of course was on young Rock,
exactly the right croc
to play the prince to
Crockafeller's Machiavelli,
one problem being unconfirmed reports
that some conservation wonks
imagined Rockadial to be a new god-king –
an avatar of sorts –
a crocodalailama of the region's underbelly.

This discovery,
inspired by young Rockadial's
miraculous recovery from coma,
and the length, strength,
and potential flick of his prodigious tail,
appeared to make him qualified to rule.
Plus, there was the finding
of auspicious flotsam in his stool
when he was sick,
stuff rumored to be grail,
and scepter,
and guitar pick.

Well, old Crockafeller'd
see about that mumbo-jumbo,
knowing, as he did,
what no one else did know,
that he was Rocky's deadbeat dad,
deserted him a dozen years ago,
when Rock was just a tad.

Nor had he ever told the crocomother,
who still believed
for her to have achieved
an offspring so recessive,
she must have mated with her brother.

CROCADOLLY

Resting on her chin,
Crocadolly watched
the last squad car drive off,
silent as a hearse.
It wasn't often that a single-engine plane,
tired of the sky, and thinking
(incorrectly) it could land on muck or worse
without much sinking,
gave it such a try.

Dolly, second of the first five reptiles to arrive,
never reckoned as she raced across the bog
she'd be in time to see
three faces through the plexi
– two human and one dog –
all looking scared, but very much alive.

Until came Rockadial, lured
from lazing in the sun
with his close chum, an alligator bird,
to crack the cockpit with his jaws
as easily as crunching crayfish claws,
and pull the white meat out;
her share, following the crocofrenzy,
one pair of lady's lips bent in a smile
(or were they upside down
and meant to be a frown?),

plus half an arm,
a hand with ring-finger intact,
but minus its gold band.
(That *Rockadial!*)

Her dopey meal got Crocadolly thinking
how thick and dark
the waters thereabouts were getting,
swamps and bogs all stinking of decay,
fish and frogs so hard to find
that crocs were forced to ruminate
on dogs and humankind.

The blame, of course,
lay at the feet of Crockafeller,
slimelord don of half the crocomafioso
in the county and beyond,
well connected in D.C.
with legislators dancing to the tunes
of crocs and alligators
bearing gold doubloons,
not to mention well-paid lobbyists
most willing to bear false witness
(favoring of course big business)
against the better interests
of their kind.

Crocadolly sighed.
What Swamptown needed
was a democratically elected
crocohero, not some fella
seeking private gain,
or prone at any moment
to be struck
by two-ton truck
or gravy train.

And then an idea came:

a U.S. senate seat for YO
was up for grabs. Why should it go
without a struggle
to some Crockafeller stooge?
One thing was clear:
If she did try to win it,
and didn't put her whole heart in it,
he'd nail her in a minute
using big bucks, lies,
and subterfuge.

ROCKADIAL IN LOVE

That wedding band he found
he gave to his dear alligator bird,
who made no fuss,
sought no commitment
(not even once referred to 'us')
just wore it on her left foot
like a trooper.

And that was fine,
yes, that was super....
Yet...there was, it seems,
another matter,
a vision that appeared
in all his recent dreams...
a certain snout, two eyes
that prettily stuck out
above the water line,
a certain tail
worth more to him, somehow,
than any scepter, pick or grail.

Her name was Crocadolly.

Crocadolly.
Just to hear it spoken
made him feel his life was broken
and the glue was Crocadolly;
made him feel like he'd been flattened
by a trolley named Desire,
helpless railroad-kill
with loins eternally on fire.

How constantly since then, day in, day out,
did Rockadial recall that lovely snout,
the way she'd chewed upon that hand
(which he had stupidly unbanded),
how she ate that smile (or frown?),
just managing to keep it down,
then wasted no time with that arm,
preferring food that still was warm.

And now had come
old Crockafeller's message,
an offer that did presage
quite a change in Rocky's lifestyle,
at the very least, a metamorphosis
from lazy lout to senator from YO.
(Plus the customary move
to Washington D.C.).

This being so, it shouldn't show,
Rock felt, a lack of cool,
or be considered cruel,
to ask the alligator bird
to give his ring back.

Ack! Oh, no! On *doing* so,
he learned (in no uncertain terms)
that she no longer *had* it.
Oh?
And when, dismayed, he blurted out:

How could you let my ring go?
the bird replied, inscrutably,
Go stuff a pink flamingo.

THE SMOKE-FILLED HILLOCK

When old Crockafeller
summoned Rocky to his hillock,
and ordered up a vat of crayfish
from his private cellar,
he learned his guest just wasn't hungry;
hadn't eaten since the feeding frenzy
following the plane disaster;
had *no* idea how long his fast would last
or just what ailed him.

I like you, boy, old Crockafeller told him
(flipped a crayfish in the air
and nailed him as he fell),
but you gotta be in good condition.
Truth to tell, you're just the croc
to beat the competition.

Like who? asked Rock, who really didn't care,
until he heard the name...heard *Crocadolly*
floating on the air.
Then he went pale, his legs gave out,
and he collapsed on belly, tail, and snout.

And there he lay, his mind awhirl,
while Crockafeller talked the afternoon away
about the Crocopotty, and it's mission
to end big government,
its taxes and restrictions
(such as eliminating trade

in threatened reptile skins).

And then, to build a fire
in the young croc's belly,
he quoted Machiavelli
who said that politics and virtue
need not mix; that in political arenas
any means is justified
to grab and then hang onto power.

And so he talked on, hour after hour,
explaining how Repelicans,
while in debates
with opposition candidates,
might make this point:
that separating politics
from morals did equate
with separating church and state
(an idea Demodiles themselves
did advocate).

Ms. Crocadolly's views,
old Crockafeller sighed,
are easy to deride
but not so easy to debate.
Which is why it's fortunate
I founded, own, and run
a tabloid called *The Crocodaily Sun*
which will always take your side
when you two tussle on the stump.

We *will?* said Rock,
whose heart went thump.

You'll find she makes her loudest racket
on questions ecological,
and every argument you make,
she will attack it. Think you can hack it?

Piece of cake, young Rock assured him.
No problemo.

Beautiful, said Crockafeller, who,
right then and there,
put foot on heart to solemnly declare:
Come water high, or water low,
I'll make you senator from YO
and off to Washington you'll go
to undermine with every vote you cast
the power of the government to tax,
plus find a way to sabotage each ruling
that subsidizes conservation
or pre-schooling.
And if you do your part,
and play it smart,
the public will grow so cynical,
that at the pinnacle of their despair
they'll cease to vote or even care.

And then you'll note
the Oval Office and the Capitol Rotunda
will weaken, topple, tear asunder,
and, as loud as thunder, fall,
and crush a century of jurisprudence,
social programs, labor unions.
And when the dust has cleared,
you'll see that power has returned
to ordinary folk like you and me,
to leave us free
to get as rich as rich can be.

You're on, said Rock, I'll run.
It sounds like fun.
And then he learned
that he was Crockafeller's son,
and that the hillock and the pool

were his to share.

Go take a dip, old Crockafeller said,
you're pretty muddy.
And then we'll have some catfish pie,
and then we'll study.

THE REVIVAL

It was a vision, it was a din;
four-hundred-twenty-seven crocs,
all freshly catechized,
re-baptized, and free of sin,
tromped muddily toward
Ye Old Revival Meeting
(first-ever of a to-be-annually-held-
and-reheld righteous revelling),
in downtown Swamptown.

On they slogged, all bellowing
their tribal greeting,
hollering their love of the All-Mighty,
Merciful, All-Knowing Crocospirit
(according to the gospel
of Horatio Crockafeller).

Hour after hour, croco-legions swarmed
out swamps and gullies,
flowed through sewers, drains, and tunnels,
over viaducts and bridges, cramming
access roads and highways,
jamming five-way intersections,
ditto driveways far and near
(seen even by the cosmonauts on Mir),
great thighs a-swishing, tails a-lashing,

slathering the muck in all directions,
till each crocodile was coated snout to bum.

CROCOHULLABALOO!
shouted headlines in *The Sun*
for weeks to come.

CROCKAFELLER'S REVERIE

Super-duper, sneered old Crockafeller,
watching from his hillock.
Swamptown's crocs, in hardly any time,
had more than doubled population 2 0 9.

It was clear his pro-life teachings
(moral preachings
that forbade the eating
of all newly hatched and barely viable,
albeit toothsome, crocodilian young),
touted piously and often
in his *Crocodaily Sun,*
had paid off two to one.
For, by so increasing population,
Crockafeller'd more than doubled
what he brought in
through extortion...uh, *taxation*,
and increased two-fold
his tabloid's circulation
(not to mention filled his bins
with luxury-grade reptile skins).

Indeed, for every Swamptown bro
who opted not to be a sinner,
and spared a baby croc
targeted to be his dinner,

he, Crockafeller, was a big-time winner.

Just look at them, he chuckled,
all so happy to be hatched
into this blighted world,
all praising *me*, the master spoiler,
envying my business smarts,
those crocs with muddy snouts
and naive hearts,
who hardly even notice
that their water isn't clean;
indeed, that almost nothing can be seen
beneath the surfaces of bogs and bayous.

Crockafeller grinned.
These fools would never know
how *he* had sinned;
that he, the town's supplier,
to make the situation dire
and send the price of water higher,
had shut off half the flow two weeks ago.

CROCAMAMA'S MISGIVINGS

Crocamama got there early
(as mothers of grown children can)
climbed the bleachers,
stretched her seven meters
on a bench, readjusted five,
and waited for the preachers,
pols, and faithful to arrive.

Soon she heard
what sounded like an alligator bird,
then dozens more,

until there were a thousand pipings,
whistlings and gripings
of a displaced flock.
And underlying all this noise
the oft-repeated shock
of foot on earth,
a mighty tromping, bellowing
and stomping, as 427 crocs
converged on downtown Swamptown.

How they thundered!
How the earth did quake
– from fear, she wondered? –
fear that ground might break,
collapse right in and shake
right down those walls
both perpendicular and round
that made the alleys
and the tunnels of the town?

One thing was certain:
With their eco-system and
their infra-structure threatened,
it was high time Swamptown
sent an eco-croc to Washington.
Not Rock, by any means;
her son was no politico
nor should he be.
(Though it was rumored
that old Crockafeller, dotty
leader of the right-wing Crocopotty,
a/k/a Repelican or C.O.P.,
had his eye on her son Rocky
for some job or candidacy.)

Well, Rock's mama had
another candidate in mind,
one with good name recognition,

zeal and charm,
eager, too, to sound alarms
concerning Swamptown's
true condition.
Crocadolly was her name and
conservation was her game.

Yes indeed, thought Crocamama,
shifting her great thighs,
a savvy gal with grassroots base
could give old Crockafeller's
boy an awesome race.

The muddy crocs did finally arrive,
treading on each other's tails,
reeling from exhaustion,
in a kind of blind elation
like robotic creatures well-prepped
for a mass indoctrination.
As Crocamama watched them
clamber up into the bleachers,
and listened to the invocation
recited by four crocopreachers,
she told herself:
Come water high or water low,
things'll hafta change
in Swamptown, YO.

AND ON THE LEFT...

Standing on the crowded dais
waiting for the multitudes to find their seats,
Crocadolly was surprised
(the word 'shocked' might be apter)
to see the name of Rockadial (that cracker!)

on the list of speakers.
She'd heard rumors he might run,
that he'd found a wealthy backer
in the right-wing owner of *The Crocodaily Sun*
(key promoter/advertiser
of Ye Old Revival Meeting),
but she'd laughed it off.
A croc who lazed all day, jaywalked,
got hit by trucks,
had clearly no sense of survival;
in fact, might make a perfect rival!

But heck, who'd want for senator
a crocodile who'd been engaged
(or so she'd heard)
to that licentious alligator bird,
who gave up scepter, grail and pick
for her, and then got jilted.
No, it was too sick.
Yet here his name was, on the list.

Crocadolly sighed.
Hers would be a lonely fight
against big money, greed,
the power of the right-wing
tabloids to mislead.
A senate race was no great pleasure,
no free ride.
To advertise her cause
she'd need the treasure
of a dozen sunken wrecks, or,
failing that, at each low tide
would have to walk along the shore
and rake the dunes,
to locate cast-up caches of doubloons.

What gave her courage
was her strong belief

that every croco-son and daughter
had the right to eat live crayfish
in clean water,
and that government,
supposedly the voter's friend,
oughter spend tax money to that end.

Crocadolly looked up at the crowd.
They were a sight, those muddy creatures
spreading outward through the bleachers,
that squirming sea of leather,
programmed to obey
old Crockafeller and his preachers,
real or lay.

Then Crocadolly turned
and from across the crowded stage
by chance did intercept the gaze
of two eyes which, when they found hers,
did melt and mist with an emotion
resembling an intense devotion.

Rockadial?
Could that stunning, mud-free croc
across the platform
be the worthless Rock?
And if so, was he running
for the very senate seat as she?

Because a candidate
with eyes so full of rapture...
and that oh, so charismatic smile...
might hope to capture
any vote – or heart –
that he went after,
Repelican *or* Demodile.

MORE MISGIVINGS

When Crocamama saw the loving look
that passed between her son and Dolly,
a lump came to her throat.
How fast they grew up!
Seems like yesterday
she'd held her baby in her jaws
to keep him safe from predators.
And now her son
had suddenly been snapped up
by that trap called love.

How the world was changing.
In *her* day mating was a chance encounter
with some stranger
(such as Rocky's unknown pa).
But today 'love' was the thing.
When possible, there even was a ring,
a golden band like one she'd seen
on that licentious alligator bird
who obviously hadn't heard
that bird and croc
(who some say shared Jurassic stock)
today can't get it on together.
Nor did that finely feathered hussy
seem to know which was a croc
and which a gator. Just *her* good luck
none took her for a flying fish
and ate her!

Her Rock in love? She had to smile.
Dolly was a Demodile
with brains and lovely leather.
A croc with truer heart and mind
Rocky couldn't hope to find.
Voting over, she and he would go
to Washington together,

Madame Senator from YO
and he her mate.

Then Crocamama looked below
at the tangled grey tableau
and wondered just which reptile
had been chosen for the Crocopotty slate.
So many muddy critters filled the dais,
it was hard to tell just who was who,
much less their bias.
And then she saw old Crockafeller,
front row center in the bleachers,
his eely features –
'specially that yellow grin –
were stretched so wide
with vile enjoyment
half the crocodentists
in the county might therein
have found employment.

But then…oh, no! A chummy look
had passed between her son
and that old crook.
And this was when
she knew beyond a doubt
her son had no idea
what Honesty was all about.

My Rock, she sighed,
is most peculiarly allied.
I wouldn't even be surprised
to learn he's running
on the Crocopotty ticket
for the senate seat from YO.
And if that's so,
I'd almost rather he had never woken
from his coma, or had croaked
a long, long time ago.

Just then a crocospeaker rose
and with his feet did pound so hard
upon the boards,
entreating the God-fearing hoards
to come to order and find seating
so that he could begin the meeting,
that they actually heeded,
got as quiet as crocs waiting
under water for some prey to seize.

And so a kind of holy silence
gripped that mob of brutish giants,
till no cough or belch or sneeze
did interrupt the speaker's greeting,
or intrude upon his reading
from a booklet of misleading
Crockafeller sophistries.

THE FIRST DEBATE

It took the best part of eight hours
for the prelims to abate,
and all this while the crowd did feed
on hot dogs of assorted breeds,
both local and imported.
Some came from Crockafeller
farms and stables, meat as fine
as ever graced the tables
of a Julia Child or Cunard Line.

And while they ate,
they quenched their thirst on Gator Juice
from fresh-squeezed alligators who,
once flayed, were diced and canned,

their well-tanned skins
then put in special bins.

They drank and drank and ate and ate.
The sky grew dark, the hour late,
but finally the moment came
that all awaited:
the one-on-one debate
by opposition candidates.

Rockadial and Crocadolly,
squinting in the spotlight,
stared at by 800 eyes,
took their places on the dais.
Then a well-known, well-liked,
very vocal crocoyokel
took the mike and posed the question:
Should all taxes be
both privatized and local?

Repealed! four hundred
crocovoters squealed.

But Rock jumped forward.
No! he pleaded.
Certain revenues *are* needed
to subsidize big corporations
and pay for lobbyists, concrete,
and bayou dredging.
What we Repelicans are pledging
is to spend your money
on necessities like these,
not let D.C. decide
what folks in Swamptown need.

Then foot on heart, young Rocky swore:
Come water high or water low,
when I to Washington do go,

I'll introduce a bill that every cent
a resident of YO is taxed
on profits and on labor
won't leave our state, but will be paid
to Crockafeller, our good neighbor,
a croc who doesn't have to guess
just who owes how much tax,
or his or her address.

Then, having sworn this, Rock did turn
and sent his burning gaze
toward Crocadolly
for her approbation and applause.

But she'd already seen the flaws
in Rocky's reasoning,
and quickly took the floor.
We crocs are anyway too poor,
she pointed out, to fall into a bracket
that the IRS can tax. With Rocky's bill,
the only one who *will*
be free of Federal taxation
– taxes that could help preserve
ecology throughout the nation –
is old Crockafeller,
a croc already rich as rich can be.
And why is he so rich?
Because he taxes us on water
found in every bog and ditch,
water which, in fact,
does not belong to him.
I say this water should be free
to each and every croc.

And then, her minute done,
and feeling she had won,
she yielded to the clock.

Young Rocky was amazed.
He had no doubt her words were true.
And suddenly Rock felt he knew
what politics was all about:
to separate from one another
lover, brother, sister, mother –
not bring them all together
in some fine cause or endeavor.

Well, there seemed no point
in speechifying half the night
until each croc collapsed from poppycock
or too much dinner.
Crocadolly clearly was the winner.
He'd argued true,
but *her* words made more sense,
and now the only thing to do
was bow to Dolly's eloquence.

Congratulations,
Rocky told her with a smile.
You won with elegance and style.
And he held out his foot.

But when her lovely foot touched his,
an overpowering emotion
like a wave out of the ocean
engulfed young Rock from tail to snout.
And all that kept the youth from passing out
was one big lusty cheer for her, his dear,
his Crocadolly, followed by applause
that seemed to sanction his surrender
to a love sublime and tender.

And then young Rocky sent
a happy grin out toward his backer.
But through the spotlights' glare
he saw the bleacher seat was bare.

Wherever Crockafeller was,
he wasn't there.

SPIN TOWN

Where had he gone?
It seems old Crockafeller'd run
to the newsroom of his *Crocodaily Sun*
to set the headlines
of tomorrow's first edition.

ROCKY WON!!!
the headline shouted.
DEMODILE CONFUSED.

Heh, heh, he laughed, amused
by his own composition.
This story'll
get things spinning.
And then he wrote an editorial
about Rock's winning.

When Swamptown crocodiles awoke
the morning after the debate,
and saw the headlines in *The Sun*,
they thought it great
that somewhere someone'd
set the record straight.
We're not too smart they opined,
as they made their muddy beds;
last night that Gator Juice
went to our heads.
Without *The Sun*
and what somebody wrote,
each one of us

would waste his precious vote.

When Crocamama saw *The Sun*
she couldn't help but feel a flash of pride
to read her boy had won.
But it was brief, for then
her anger and her indignation rose.
Who does old Crockafeller
think he is, to feed us lies like those?
No croc attending that debate,
no matter how much juice he drank
or canine ate,
could fail to note
that Crocadolly earned his vote.

And so she went to see the 'loser',
to, if need be, disabuse her
of all feelings of rejection
caused by someone's cunning bid
to micro-manage the election.

ON THE BEACH

The surf was grey,
the mermaids singing each to each.
She found poor Crocadolly
walking on the beach,
dejected and alone,
scratching at each dune and stone,
but finding few doubloons
for all her trying.
Dolly'd read *The Sun*
and there was no denying
she was up against
a tough political machine,

operated by a croc as mean
as mean could be.

But Dolly, Crocamama said,
my Rocky just adores you.
He'd as soon be dead
as let you go or let you lose.

Don't bet on it, said Dolly.
If Rocky had to choose
between that bird and me,
the senate and his dad…

His *dad*, cried Crocamama.
Who would *that* be?

But Crocadolly shut her snout.
If Crocamama hadn't heard
the gossip bruited all about,
how could *she* ever tell her
Rocky's dad was said to be
old Crockafeller?

But Crocadolly's silence
seemed to scream the unsaid truth.
Suddenly the name of her ex-lover
hit poor Crocamama like a manhole cover
rolling forty miles an hour.
And though she felt
that something in her died,
which may have been her pride,
she opted to make no response,
at least not for the nonce.

SONG OF THE MERMAIDS

What were the mermaids singing?
Songs of love, of course,
and warnings of rough seas
and dangerous rocks.
They sang of love
between two star-crossed crocs,
for they could see
(as ungrammatical as it might be)
that she loved him
as much as he loved she.

But there were dangers
for the two; reptiles who
had far too much at stake
in things political
to care how far they went,
or be self-critical
about which rules they bent.

The mermaids sang of love,
of rocky coasts, of death and dying.
And was that sea spray on their cheeks?
Or were they crying?

A BUTTERFLY IN PEKING

Two more big debates did follow,
and all agreed that Crocadolly'd won,
until they read the morning *Sun*.
This was frustrating for Dolly.
Her dire warnings and expoundings
on the state of their surroundings
were for naught.

Swamptown crocs quite simply bought
whatever nonsense Crockafeller wrote.
And what was worse,
he had Rocky in his purse.

What could she do
to separate those two?
Perhaps put out the word
that till *The Sun* did shine a probing beam
on Swamptown muck,
she'd have no further truck
with Rocky. So she did it,
though it broke her heart to shut him out.
Because she loved that Rock,
a croc as dear as dear could be –
a croc so shy he'd not yet
dared approach her off the stump,
much less declare his love,
the silly chump.

Well, it might work.
And anyway, a gentle nudge
could do no harm,
just sound a very faint alarm,
not cause the world to go berserk.

TORNADO SKIES OVER YO

When Rocky heard his dearest treasure
looked upon him with displeasure,
he hurried straight to Crockafeller.

Dad, he said,
I'm too in love with Dolly
to continue to oppose her.

I and everyone who knows her
find her reasoning well-grounded,
all her arguments well-founded,
her expoundings well-expounded,
and everything expressed
with style and grace.
In short, I'd like to quit the race.

Crockafeller was astounded.
His son in love with *Crocadolly?*
Could Rock's recent melancholy,
his lackluster conduct in debate,
plus his strange predisposition
to capitulate, result from love
of one he ought to hate?

But boy, you're doing great.
You've won each contest, every single one.
You *must* have read that in *The Sun*.
Hey, voting's just a week away,
the ballot's printed.
Promise dad you'll be there with him,
nothing stinted, on Election Day.

Well, thought Rocky,
one week's not a big concession.
Once the polls have closed,
no matter which of us has won,
I'll pop the question.
Okay, dad, he told him
after pondering a minute.
If you want me to, I'll run,
but my heart's not in it.

CROCAMAMA'S CONFRONTATION

I'm playing patriarch today,
grinned Crockafeller,
noting who was climbing up his hillock.
Come on, he called, and take a load off.
Rest your tush.
But Crocamama,
scorning his false greeting,
said she hadn't come to beat
around the bush.

If you think Rock's your blood relation,
you should honor him enough
to set him free of filial
and feudal obligation.
Let him wed in peace, and work with her
to keep our species viable.
I'm sure that even *you* must see
that you and he now disagree
on every subject of debate.

Old gal, you're certifiable,
laughed aloud the evil croc.
Don't worry about Rock.
I'll see the boy obeys his pa.

Crocamama set her jaw.
We Demodiles intend to win.
Repelicans will take it on the chin
unless they smarten up real fast.

But then she paused, aghast,
to see he wore a golden band
around one tooth,
the very ring her son
had given to that bird
(whom, incidentally, none had seen

or heard in weeks).
What did it mean? An avian donation
to a right-wing crocoboss,
or sloppy flossing following a snack?

I'm off now, Crocamama said,
and won't be back.
But listen to the words of she
who soon will be your daughter,
and do what any decent
news-croc oughter:
direct *The Sun*'s bright beams
to probe what's rotten in the state of YO.

Like in your dreams,
old Crockafeller growled.
Now do us both a favor,
you sententious cow,
and *go*.

THE CELLAR

Below the grassy surface of a hillock,
in a dark and dankish crayfish cellar,
stood a cage with one bird in it.
Minute after boring minute,
hour after day,
she watched the crayfish vats
and wondered why fish looked
as odd as they,
and why they called them cray.

It comes from Middle French *crevis*,
an elderly acquaintance
in the corner told her,

though French is not my field of expertise.
Then, getting bolder,
he went on, But tell me why
you call yourself an alligator bird,
a name I've never heard.

Replied the bird,
It's a question of poetic meter;
alligator bird sounds neater
than crocodile bird,
a/k/a African plover,
which is what I really am,
my species no doubt smuggled over.
But *that* name, like the one
my mother gave me,
is poetically unscannable.

And what might that name be?

She called me Annabel,
Annabel Lee, a bunch
of syllables and stresses
useless to an honest poet.

How well I know it,
sighed the man,
and how often *I've* despaired
at having *my* name and addresses,
PhD and MS's
poetically impaired.
My name, you see, is J.A. Prufrock,
and I'm a homeless ornithologist.

At this, the alligator bird,
tipping one eye toward the corner,
asked him was he sleeping there on gunny
'cause he'd lost his job and money?

Just so, said he.
As wing-ed species go extinct
there's less work for the likes of me,
whose specialty
is birdies having vital signs.
When pulse and breathing go away
I find I've nothing more to say.
It's at such times
an honest ornithologist resigns.

The captive bird let out a sigh.
It's good to hear
that *some*where out there
honesty's alive and kicking;
the evil croc who put me in this cage
deserves a licking.

Dr. Prufrock could not believe his ears.
You say a *croc* is holding you?
A *crocodile*?
A beast that lives one hundred years,
that grows nine meters long,
and has a jaw so strong and big
that it can down a full-sized pig?

That's right, the bird replied,
that's Crockafeller to a T,
a croc as mean as mean can be,
and big as he is mean.

Then, panicked by a mortal dread,
J.A. Prufrock said,
I-better-leave-before-I'm-seen.

But it already was too late
to latch onto a different fate.
In minutes he was found and drowned
and served up on a dinner plate.

And with his vital signs away
he found he had no more to say.
And though he wanted to resign,
they washed him down
with Beaujolais.

A CROCOSITION

Next to Crockafeller on his hillock
stood a cage with one bird in it.
Minute after minute,
with utter disregard,
the aged reptile let escape
a sulfurous petard.

Ha! That bloody feed
had been exactly what he'd needed
to concentrate his mind on future deeds,
deeds as gory and perverse
as ever did enslime the lining
of a coffin or a hearse –
deeds to foment dread
and cause some dead
among the opposition,
all without the least blame
or suspicion falling on his head.

Then, turning to the bird he said,
Now listen up, for here's a proposition
that you can't refuse,
if ever you expect to lose
this cage and fly off free.

And she, of course, did listen,
for the air and breeze

were clear and bright
and sunlight glistened
on a zillion birds and gators,
crocs and frogs,
cavorting in the muddy bogs.
Indeed, this chance to fly away
provoked such yearning
that her heart was burning
with suspense to hear
what he would say.

And then he told her that she'd play
the role of messenger between two lovers,
like that Friar and that Nurse,
who once upon a time in far Verona
helped turn love's sweet song
into a curse.
Then, scraping the gold band
from off his tooth,
he said, Here, give her this,
and she'll believe *he* sent you
and assume you speak the truth.

APPROACHING E-DAY

Campaigns were drawing to a close;
Election Day was near.
Three dozen alligator birds,
midnight volunteers,
hopped from croc to sleeping croc
and whispered '*Dolly*' in their ears.
This subliminal campaigning
was a last ditch effort,
and a desperate one,
to stop a criminal from claiming

victory for his son.

Rockadial, who didn't care who won or lost,
couldn't wait for the election to be done with,
wanted just to find his Dolly,
lie out in the sun with her,
and pop the question.

He knew his father
couldn't long resist his bride.
He'd soon set right-wing politics aside,
and then all three would go together to D.C.
and live in simple harmony,
making sure by making laws
that crocs stayed off the Interstate,
avoided poachers' traps,
found ways to resist drought,
in short, insure that crocs did not die out,
for that's what life was all about.

The week without his darling Dolly
passed as slowly as a year.
But when election eve arrived
Rock's spirits rose. Tomorrow,
when the polls had closed,
he'd go to Dolly and propose.

THE BETRAYAL

Election eve, old Crockafeller
opened the cage door.
Fly straight and true,
he told the alligator bird,
and when you get there, do
exactly as I told you to,

remembering the while,
that if you flee, or try to trick me
with your cunning or your guile,
you'll never lunch again
upon a sunning crocodile.

She had a hunch he wasn't kidding,
that she'd better do his bidding
or she'd rue the day.
So, hopping from the cage,
she slipped the golden band
upon her foot, and flew away.

It was already growing dark
when she found Crocadolly
in a pond within a park,
watching children play.
She hadn't come there to aggress them,
pull them under or ingest them.
She yearned only to caress them
for she had no babies of her own.

The alligator bird flew down
and perched on Crocadolly's head.
I've brought a message
from a friend, she said,
who wants to meet you right away.
And then she paused,
because it wasn't easy
to betray another creature,
even her, that very croc
who'd made her own romance with Rock
a jealous mockery.

Crocadolly's heart beat fast.
If the bird spoke true, at last
she'd be together with her love.
But wasn't this the very bird

she'd heard had made a contribution
to the right-wing C.O.P?

Some say I did, the alligator bird agreed,
but don't be miffed. I swear it was no gift.
You see, one day I lost a golden band
that Crockafeller found upon the sand.
He gave it to his son, who's given it to me
to give to you by way of proof
that what I'm saying is the truth.
And taking off the ring, she held it out
beyond the end of Dolly's snout.

I trust you, Crocadolly said.
Where does he want to meet?

In that same bog, the bird replied,
where one fine day a Cessna
fell from high above
and landed at your feet;
the day he fell in love.

Her words were gracious and disarming,
but at the same time quite alarming.
For, since that day a holy lot
of humans seeking souvenirs
had visited that spot.
And once those piggish tourists made it
ecologically degraded,
poachers came and set out traps and snares.
If Rocky went there unawares,
he might be trapped or shot.

I'd better warn him, Dolly said.
Then, slipping the gold band upon her tooth,
she thanked the alligator bird and hurried off.

For what I've done, the bird lamented,

there are no words.
And then she saw, as if presented in a dream,
a flock of alligator birds
alighting on the backs of dozing crocs.
How strange,
for next she seemed to hear the name
of *Dolly* floating like a ghostly mist
upon the moonlit scene.

And if this was an omen,
what did the omen mean?

ELECTION DAY

Election Day dawned warm and drear.
High voter turnout was expected,
though some had become disaffected
by the dirty politicking.
Even before seven-thirty,
crocs from every part of YO
(several screaming and some kicking),
trickled into downtown Swamptown.
There they learned
the way to indicate their choice
was not by ballot, but by voice;
votes were bellowed
and the decibels were tallied.
At first Rock seemed to be ahead,
then Crocadolly rallied.

And that was fine, yet Rock was worried.
Eager to see Dolly, he had hurried
into town that morning.
When by noon she hadn't come,
he wondered why. Where could she be?

Suddenly a bird lit on his head.
Rocky, the bird said, it's me,
your former friend. I've come to tell you....
But the bird could not continue,
could not say what Crockafeller'd
told her to relate:
that Dolly wanted nevermore to see him,
and had left the state.
She knew that Rock would hate her
for the part she'd played,
but now, unable to keep lying,
she blurted out,
Oh Rocky, Crocadolly's dying.

Where is she? Rocky cried.

And so she told him,
knowing that if Crocadolly died
no creature of the earth or sky above
would ever again win his trust
or love.

FINDING DOLLY

Without a moment's hesitation
Rock turned and disappeared
into the vegetation.
The alligator bird flew overhead,
relating all the deeds that led up
to this tragedy. But Rocky
hardly heeded what she said.

Wary of the hidden traps,
as he approached the fatal bog,

Rockadial picked up a log
and held it out between his jaws
to set them off and clear the way.

And so he rapidly advanced, until the bird,
who had a better view,
said softly, There she is.
And then he saw her too,
half hidden in some reeds,
one leg taken in a trap.

Rockadial approached her gently.
Oh, Dolly, Rocky said,
I have to save you.
If I can't, I'll never leave you.

I believe you,
Crocadolly told him,
wishing she could kiss and hold him.
Rock, I love you, but beware,
there are poachers everywhere.
You, as senator from YO,
will do a lot of good
for crocs throughout the state,
but if you don't go soon,
it soon may be too late.

But Rocky was indifferent to his fate.
Her life was far more threatened than his own.
He saw that even if his mighty jaws
could separate the claws of steel
that gripped her leg,
it would cause her greater pain.
Her life hung by a thread,
and it was plain to both of them
he could not save her.

O do not die! Rock would have said,

could he have paraphrased John Donne,
for I shall hate
all living creatures so
when thou art gone,
that thee I shall not celebrate
when I remember, thou wast one.

But what he did say was,
Oh, Dolly, if you die, then soon or late
I'll kill the reptiles
who have brought you to this fate.
Were I to live a hundred years,
how could I legislate
with a heart so full of hate?
And then he gently placed his length
beside her, close as close could be,
so she'd absorb his love and energy.

Just then a shout was heard.
Ecologists are coming! cried the alligator bird.
The same you met after your coma.

A desperate hope seized Rock.
They'll take you to a vet, he said.

But Dolly knew before the sun had set
she would be dead.
Don't let them touch me, Rock.
I'd rather die with you beside me
in this bog, than with the kindest strangers,
be they conservationists or rangers.

Her words did break his heart,
but Rocky understood.
So as the people came their way
he raised his head
and bellowed out a warning.

Hey, look! one cried,
that female croc is in a trap,
and that big male is trying to protect her.
She'll die unless we find a way
to make him leave so we can save her.

Just then a man appeared,
a lethal weapon on his shoulder.
Great! I trapped one, he rejoiced.
These crocodiles are getting bolder.
Some days ago
a small plane landed in this bog
and reptiles just like those
ate pilot, passenger, and dog.
You say that male's protecting her?
Let's see if Supercroc moves faster
than a speeding bullet;
and so saying, raised his AK-47,
aimed and fired.
In the din that followed
forty rounds pierced Dolly's side
and she expired.

But before the sound had faded,
he had found that men do better
on dry ground than under water
where a power greater than a locomotive
brought him in a single bound.

I hope they get the sucker,
was his final thought
before he drowned.

THE AFTERMATH

Waiting in his newsroom for his plan to hatch,
old Crockafeller came across
a worrisome dispatch;
two deaths had just occurred
within that bog where he had set his plot.
And then came word
one candidate was shot,
the other on the run.

And suddenly his son
was in the limelight,
rumored to be carrying a gun,
and ordered shot on sight.
And next, he heard,
from a snitchy stringer-bird,
that Rocky had been told about *his* role
in Crocadolly's death,
and had sworn to get him.

Does he think I'll bloody *let* him?
Crockafeller snarled.
Just because my son's
prodigious whip of tail and snap of jaw
have caused that whippersnapper
to be hunted by the law,
does not imply he's any threat
to his well-bodyguarded pa.

Then, having put a contract out
on Rocky's feathered friend,
Crockafeller hurried downtown,
where he found the voting not yet at an end.
For though the voters knew
one candidate was dead,
and one had fled –
in what a New York newspaper

would (incorrectly) call
a stunning dual defection –
what *no* one knew, was what to do
to stop the damned election.

Then Crockafeller said, Upon reflection,
I feel that I can help you
through this sorry situation.
Make *me* your senator from YO
and off to Washington I'll go
to write new legislation
that will benefit our state.

And so they gave him every vote,
despite the screams
of one despairing croco-mom
who told him where he *ought* to go,
and not just in his dreams.

THE AFTERMATH - PART DEUX

It was the worst day of his life,
and looked to be the last.
Beside each bog and ditch, the blast
of rifle shots resounded.
Crocs that looked like Rockadial
(and many did, to untrained eyes)
were killed by strangers,
guys with guns who felt
they had a bona fide excuse
to unloose fire power.
Conservationists and rangers
worked to stop them, and,
about the twilight hour,
calm descended on the land.

Shortly after dark,
Rock found Crocamama
in the lake within the park
where Crocadolly used to watch
as children played.
It's here my Dolly was betrayed,
he told her bitterly,
and then, dry-eyed,
related how she'd died.

Oh, Rock, she said,
it would help you if you cried.

I will not cry, said Rockadial.
Not yet, not yet.

But Crocamama did,
and when she'd done
she told him Crockafeller
was en route to Washington,
to take the senate seat
that he or Dolly would have won.

Dad's history, said Rock.
I'm on my way.

Well, be real careful, son,
and take these gold doubloons.
They're still a little sandy,
but will surely come in handy
in a town like Washington.

But Rock refused. Said he,
There's nothing gold can buy
that teeth and will as strong as mine
cannot obtain.

Except, she smiled,
a ticket for the train.

So he accepted one doubloon
(with some chagrin),
then chucked her on the chin
and kissed her snout,
'cause that's what moms
were all about.

CROCKAFELLER IN D.C.

When Horatio Crockafeller
slithered from the train,
he heard tremendous cheers.
He hadn't been to Washington
in over eighty years,
yet was a legend in the place,
a lobbyist, a donor;
to politicians of the right,
king maker and dethroner.

So when he left the train that night,
he found a city of delight.
The Mall was filled with gold balloons
that shone as brightly as doubloons,
while marching bands with big bassoons
played stirring patriotic tunes.

And this was all for him, for *him,*
the senator elect,
who'd staged an upset victory
to give his grateful party
a congressional majority.

Old Crockafeller grinned.
How different from
his first time in this town.
Back then he was a yokel
from a backwater called YO,
who didn't even know
when staying at a Washington hotel
one didn't eat the desk clerk
or his bell,
or the bellhop, for that matter.
Nor, could this callow youth
have guessed a hotel might express
extreme displeasure,
even threaten *him*, a guest,
with criminal arrest
like any common felon,
were he to eat the waiter
after ordering up melon.

Well, since those days
he'd opted to remain behind the scenes,
and, in the century's late teens,
concealed his greed, intentions
and ambition
while supporting women
in their fight for prohibition.
This artfully successful,
Constitution-changing ruse
earned him fortunes in the '20's
through the sale of bootleg booze.

In the '30's, auctioneering
helped him buy up bankrupt farms,
while his post-war profiteering
was black-market surplus arms.
No one in the '50's gave
more money to the Klan;
in the '60's Crockafeller was

the croc they called The Man.
In the next two decades, takeovers
and mergers were his thing,
while the '90's found him dealing
in hard drugs and publishing.

It seemed quite fitting to him, then,
to come to Washington again
to start a new endeavor on
the eve of the millennium.

So say goodbye to bogs and dunes,
said Crockafeller to his goons.
Then he, with local croco-mobsters,
through the wee-est morning hours,
quaffed champagne, smoked big cigars,
and dined on caviar and lobsters.

ON THE TRAIN

All through the endless hours on the train,
Rock couldn't sleep. Again, again, again,
a dark, reptilian force,
like some rough beast
from out an ancient lair,
revisited the awful actions of that day,
and with its nails did etch deep in his soul
a track that led to vengeance,
not despair.

As for the moments
in between those hellish crossings,
marked by turnings and by tossings,
into memories obscene,
Rock lay as still and dim

as some uprooted tree trunk, log, or limb.
The roar and oscillations of the train
made mind and body numb,
while Crocadolly's image in his brain
was like a small, bright sun
inside a universe of pain.

Her musky scent, a sweet refrain
that kept the song of her alive,
played on. No other scent
would ever in him work that miracle
to turn a blood so cold to fire,
make whole marshes redolent
of Crocadolly, and desire.

On Rocky's back perched one
who shared in petit parallel
his heartbreak and his ire.
It was that alligator bird,
another victim of the fate
stage-managed by a croc
who didn't hesitate
to murder and manipulate.
She felt her life and self-respect
had both been wrecked
by happenings beyond
her comprehension,
or her power to affect.

So she had sworn,
no matter what the risk,
to stay by Rocky's head,
give help and never run,
until the foe was dead
and victory was won.

ROCKADIAL IN D.C.

Rock arrived in Washington at dawn,
and it was clear
a party had been going on.
Large tents still stood upon the Mall,
and strewn about the monuments
to well-loved former presidents
were soda cans and fast food wrappers.
Meditating hundred-lappers
ran around a tidal pool
where Rocky stopped to take a dip.

Just then he heard a cheerful cry
and saw some men go jogging by.
One wore a smile of good intent
and, yes, it was the president.
Seeing him was such a thrill
that then and there did Rocky swear:
Come water high or water low,
if I this nightmare do survive,
and somehow live to thirty-five,
I'll run for U.S. president,
my platform: the environment.
Thus Dolly's message will live on
and that will be her monument.

You ought to find a sauna,
said some stranger standing near.
That's where the other crocs all go,
to warm their blood and rub their snouts
with top politicos from out
the fifty states, and YO.
Now, if you wonder how I know....

Oh, let me guess,
broke in the alligator bird.
You are a herpetologist.

Just so, replied the man, impressed.
My name is Best,
and I am usually addressed,
by those who know, as Dr. Best.
But here I think we have digressed.
You see, since YO became a state
(thanks to the thousands of doubloons
a certain reptile did donate
to some key legislative races),
throughout D.C. there's been a spate
of truly downhome crocofaces,
which to me has been a boon.

But you look starved, said Dr. Best,
and there are rivers all about....

Said Rock, I don't need
frogs or trout.
Enough is on my plate
to sate a dozen crocs like me.
Then, stepping from the pool, he
quickly found the scent
of Crockafeller near a tent
and followed it to a hotel,
approached the desk
and rang the bell.

When Crockafeller heard
a croc and bird
were asking for him at Reception,
he sent down word
that he was resting,
but would meet them
at the mouth of Rock Creek Park
in the hour before dark,
adding, they should come alone.

It doesn't matter,
Rock assured the alligator bird
(beside herself with apprehension).
Since I alone can fight my fight,
it might as well be fought tonight.
Then he, to ease her tension,
used the change from his doubloon
to buy some food
and rent a private sauna room.
And there they stayed
the long day through,
waiting for the rendezvous.

SHOWDOWN AT ROCK CREEK

An hour before dark,
at the mouth of Rock Creek Park,
five crocodiles did meet
in a four-to-one-croc distribution.
An alligator bird was also there,
scared, but filled with resolution.
She'd already made a flight
around the park, to see,
before the fall of night,
what she could see.
She saw a playground and a zoo,
a bridle path and stable too,
and now was perched up in a tree.

Said Crockafeller to his limo driver,
Come and get us in an hour.
But while you're gone, re-stock your bar
with fifty pounds of caviar,
a dozen magnums of champagne
and several buckets of chow mein.

And then he turned to Rockadial.

You seem to think, the old croc said,
that you're a threat upon my life.
If this continues, I'll see to it
you and your bird friend do rue it.

But when their eyes met, Rocky saw
his struggle now was with a force
much greater than his pa.
It was a struggle in himself
with something he had never had
to face before:
an ancient, archetypical taboo,
passed down through blood into
the dark subconscious
of a vast collective mind.
It said: *A crocodile must never kill
another of its kind.*

And it was plain as plain could be
the only vertebrate on earth that *did* this act
that every other species did abhor,
that regularly killed its kind
in private and in war,
and even celebrated this
in poetry and lore, was man.

I think you'll find,
Rock said, that I have other plans
to deal with you.

His father smiled.
And may I ask what those plans are?

Said Rock, I'll drive you off so far
from all your seats of power
and great wealth,

which were amassed through
murder, lies, and stealth,
that none will ever hear of you again.
Although I swear, if killing you would
bring my Dolly back to me,
I wouldn't hesitate to put away
my honor and my pride,
and break the strongest taboo of them all,
the one called patricide.

Strong words, sneered Crockafeller.
Don't forget, my son, to get at me
you'll have to fight not one but three.
And I do prophesy
that they will shrug off every punch,
and clean your clock
and eat your lunch,
and hang you out to dry.
And when they're done
I'll print your obit in *The Sun*.

One thing was certain,
all three crocs in question
were the most redoubtable
that Rock had ever seen.
Their jaws were cruel,
their eyes were mean,
their leather tough.
From snout to tail
they were the stuff
of which bad dreams are made.
Yet Rockadial was unafraid.
He'd suffered far too much,
and felt he had already lost
more than his life was worth
– his joy in sky and sea and earth –
to fear to die.

And so Rock faced the three
and told them honestly:
To stop me you will have to kill me.
But I warn you, it will not be easy.
Make my day, and try.

On hearing this, the goons looked shocked
and took young Rockadial aside.
Us *kill* you? Don't you know
that since ten million years ago
we crocs have had a rule
against the killing of our kind?
If while we were protecting *him*,
we were obliged to butcher *you*,
we'd surely break that old taboo,
and that's one thing we'd never do.

Thought Rock, I truly fear,
despite their honorable words,
these crocs are insincere.
For aren't these three the same
who at Ye Old Revival Meeting
squeezed those gators till they cried,
then flayed their skins before they died,
to put in special bins?

So, Rock, they said, don't worry about us.
Do your darndest to the guy
and be our guest.
We three feel blessed
that we can leave him here with you
while we head home.
For, though we never let it show,
we miss our wives and kids in YO.

Then off they went, but just as soon
as they were out of sight
they climbed into a limousine

and sped off in the night.
Because, it seems,
the three were in the pay
of mafiosi
who had told them to betray
their croco-boss
in a classic double-cross.

I hear you fellows played
old Crockafeller's curtain song
like virtuosi,
they were told by one old croco-don,
reclining with dark glasses on.
When Rockadial starts in with him,
he'll *wish* that he was dead and gone.

And then he smiled
at his three hick-town goons,
and promised them enough doubloons
to make them wildly rich.
And then he bade his chauffeur
take a turn-off down a road along a ditch
where they were bound with tape
from tail to nape.

And when they asked the reason why,
his irrefutable reply
was: Life's a bitch and then you die.

At which the car door opened wide
and all three were propelled outside.
And there for two long weeks they lay,
and then were found, and hauled away.

CROCKAFELLER'S FATE

When Crockafeller realized
that the current distribution
was a one-on-one,
and one of these a mean old croc,
and one his gallant, unforgiving son,
he knew his time had come.

Get on with it, he said.
What will you have me do?

We'll walk a bit, said Rock.
I hear that there's a zoo....

A *zoo*, the old croc cried
with breaking voice.
I'll never go into a zoo.
To be confined and on display
is *worse* than being dead.

But Crockafeller had no choice.
With Rockadial behind him
and the bird upon his head,
they walked the long park through,
and at the very minute that it opened,
found the zoo.

The directors were ecstatic
when they saw the monster croc,
a species that was lacking
in their fine reptilian stock.

But I'm the senator from YO,
cried Crockafeller angrily.
If you dare lay a hand on me,
I'll see you lose your subsidy.

The directors hesitated,
for if what he said was true,
they could not put him in their zoo.

Just then a herpetologist spoke up.
I understand your grave concern,
regarding this croc's claim,
said he, for to the untrained eye
most crocofaces look the same,
especially a father and his son.
But I will gladly certify
the senator from YO
is *Rocky* Crockafeller,
and not Horatio.

And so they led old Crockafeller off
and put him in a kind of glass aquarium.
In time he proved a popular display,
and people came from miles away
to stare at him.

EPILOGUE

The next day Rock was seated
on the left side of the aisle,
for he had changed his party
and become a Demodile.
The alligator bird,
who'd slept over at the zoo
(a guest of their Bird Resource Center),
had some babies with another plover
who was housed there too.
When their fledglings left the nest,
she gave her mate a peck goodbye
and flew to Rocky's side.

Then this croc and alligator bird,
who'd been through bitter times together,
worked on Dolly's legacy
with no let-up whatsoever.
In May they called a croco-march,
supporting eco-legislation.
Reptiles came to Washington
from every corner of the nation
(though tallies of their numbers
differed ten-to-one
between the Pulitzer-Prize-winning
Crocadolly Sun
and that conservative, infernal
tabloid called *The Wall Street Journal*).

Six years went by and Rock
was re-elected in a landslide.
When he reached the age of thirty-five
(by then his father, mom, and bird had died),
Rock ran for president, and won,
and four years later won again.

By then, he had inherited
his father's wealth.
With still a long, long time to live,
and millions of doubloons to give
through numerous foundations,
and since he had no daughter and no son,
Rock became
the world's first dynasty of one.

EPILOGUE - PART DEUX

As the century wore on,
Rock saw with sorrow
where the world was heading;
despite much trying,
human populations everywhere
were spreading,
displaced creatures dying.

In 2027, while politicians worldwide
worried about re-election,
the last surviving Bengal tiger, lacking habitat
and looked on as a dangerous pest,
took a bullet in the chest.
(After which her priceless skin
was put into a special bin.)

In 2032, the last black rhino,
born and raised inside a zoo,
was murdered for his horn, which,
powdered into finest dust
was stored in special tins,
and sold as aphrodisiacs
to Nipponese insomniacs.

In 2034, the two remaining forests,
one in Argentina, one El Salvador,
were burned, so that a burger czar
could raise some hay to graze his herds.
Indeed, the cattle grazed so well,
that two years later all that land,
where once did dwell
tree nymphs and rarest birds,
was nothing more than sand, more sand,
and cattle turds.

In 2045, starving human populations,

coughing in the noxious air,
tried penetrating other nations.
Those not shot by border guards,
learned to savor
every edible they found:
tree sloths, baboons,
even maggots in the ground
(which soon returned the favor).

In 2048, global warming
caused such floods and drought,
that half the continents were
under water, half dried out.

Then, in 2053, in places like
the Vineyard, Costa Rica and Nepal,
the last surviving native species
lost their war with tourist feces.

EPILOGUE - FIN

So the years went by,
and, in 2085, old Rocky was the last
remaining crocodile alive. One day,
feeling that his time had come,
he wrote an editorial
for the final issue of *The Sun*.

We tried, he wrote, we truly tried.
Perhaps our efforts did,
for one brief moment, help restrain
the tide of muck and murk
that has destroyed our world.
I think we must concede
(if 'we' obtains,

and anyone to read this column
still remains),
that many animals, and mankind,
had a certain flaw.

From a million years ago
until, let's say, the year of 1925,
this defect did appear to be a strength
that probably evolved to help
all creatures of a hostile world survive.
But later, it did aid the human race
to grow and multiply
and eat the whole wide world alive.

The defect? Call it greed,
self-interest, lust for power;
the Age of Politics that it did breed,
was not our planet's finest hour.

Then Rocky signed his name
and went outside
to watch the sun go down
upon the old, abandoned theme park
where once jolly humans,
dressed like dogs and mice, did romp.
It was a place that formerly
had been a swamp,
with bogs and marshes deep and wet
and scented with the musk
of Crocadolly.
Now the sun had set, and it was dusk,
and those enchanted ponds
a long, long time ago had dried.

Then Rock lay down upon his hillock,
and he cried.

KROH

*The Greening
of a Small Planet*

CONTENTS

PART THREE: THE RETURN

THE PROLOGUE

Not so long ago from now
a space ship went from Earth to Kroh,
a planet long ignored by one and all.

For though it lay
but one light week away,
and was inhabited
by creatures thought to be
intelligent as men,
whose air was oxygen,
who lived, like us, on land and sea,
Kroh failed to stir our curiosity
as did the moon and Mars.

Those rocky spheres among our stars,
each with vistas sharp and spare,
peopled by a greenish race
that made their lair
in every crevice and canal
and rode their UFO's
like perfect hellions,
abducting dozens of Roswellians,
remained our endlessly
renewable frontiers.

Whereas Kroh, a planet reckoned at
a billion population,
its rocks worn smooth
by creatures walking, and some sitting,
this late into its faunal evolution
lacked baseball parks and football fields
and evidence of air pollution.

On the night Kroh was discovered
(by a boy named Marvin Kroh),
the planet, swimming in a distant sky,

was contacted by hackers
and sent back this strange reply:
Yeah sure. Feel free.
Come right on up. BYOB.

Let's fight that bunch of losers,
cried the pundits on TV;
send those tedious non-boozers
to a place called History.

Smiled the right-wing politicians,
This is when it makes good sense
to take billions out of Schooling
to bestow upon Defense.
But alas, their legislation,
like an innocent mosquito,
got slapped down late one Friday
by a presidential veto.

So after that the journalists
and congress did agree
they'd better forget war
and keep their waking hours free
to monitor the Dow and Nasdaq
and the S&P,
plus those emerging markets
and Japan's economy.

The years went by until one night
a young teacher of astronomy,
wishing on the evening star
for his grant to be approved,
realized that if making money and not war
was what man was put here for,
astronomy could lead the nation.

In an instant he'd rewritten
his entire application,

named his project
'Inter-Global Market Hunting'.
The result? Was given funding
that surpassed all expectation
to construct a modest space ship
and take experts off to Kroh,
to learn if that small planet
was politically ripe,
its currencies robust enough
and of a stripe
to enter into trade relations
with the Earth and all its nations.

His blue-ribbon Delegation
was a rainbow; had some humans,
had a Duck from Washington, D.C.,
two Crocodiles from YO,
and what they all were feeling
ranged from horror to delight
to find themselves en route to Kroh
one starry, starry night.

PART ONE:

THE JOURNEY

THE SPACE SHIP

It was a ship designed for speed
and cheap to build.
To keep the voyagers and crew
from floating, as the ship flew
far from fields of gravitation,
there was Velcro.
This allowed the Delegation
(with that Duck, who wore it on his feet)
to sit and stick to any seat
(especially the toilet,
without concern they might
float off a bit, and miss, and soil it).

The living space had been equipped
for passengers of every genus,
from the longest, lowest, fattest
to the uprightest and leanest.
For those who liked to watch
galactic stars shoot by,
panoramic windows lined each side.
And even in the rest room at the rear,
a porthole underneath one vent
let a passenger observe,
while seated on his Velcroed bum,
the starry way that he had come
the whole time that he went.

(Reader, for these earthy details
we are sorry.
In the future precious few,
and only those unarguably true,
will be included in our story.
Normally upon these pages
strict propriety prevails;
this is not *Candide*, *The Simpsons,*
or *The Canterbury Tales*.)

THE DELEGATION

The members of the Delegation,
each aboard by invitation,
were all Americans.
For congress felt, and rightly so,
since voter taxes
underwrote the expedition,
and our Astronomer began it,
U.S. interests should outweigh
all other on the planet.

The humans came from different fields
and were as many as sixteen.
We will not try to list them here,
for we are not inclined to waste our time
attempting to make sixteen
wildly different occupations rhyme
when, anyway, they'll soon appear.
(If still you will insist
that we reveal this nonsense,
refer you to this volume's CONTENTS.)

And then there were those frightened Crocs
who couldn't comprehend their luck.

And then there was that Duck.

THE DUCK

The Duck from Washington, D.C.,
a world-renowned celebrity,
was not a mallard, canvasback,

or green-winged teal.
No, Sam was hatched
a simple barnyard fowl,
all white, with yellow bill.

And yet this ordinary duck
had had a marvelous career.
Beginning at an eastern daily
as a lowly copy duck,
Sam Donal waddled
up the ranks, dabbling
in all kinds of muck.
His big break came the night
that he reported (live)
one thousand Russian tanks
were speeding down I-95.
This information did so terrify the nation
– and his tears of fright so charmed it –
overnight he was a hero.

So what if he was wrong in his reporting?
So what if those nocturnal streams
were only armored trucks transporting
foreign-made components
to a striking auto plant?
So *what* if Sam had later to recant?
From this one happy slip
his fame and name would come.

And what a name it was!
By blind dumb luck,
just one week past
he'd changed his name
from Donal to McDonalduck,
a moniker more fit by far
for one become a superstar.

The offers that now came his way

were legion, and he grabbed
the best job in the region:
anchor Duck at CBA.
His yearly pay?
Eight million bucks.
Sam had become, in short,
the wealthiest of ducks.
Still, feeling he had more to say,
and having free time in the day,
he took a second job as
White House correspondent Duck
at half again the pay,
became a D.C. resident,
and soon was seen on every TV screen
quacking questions at the president.

Yet this assignment
taking him to outer space
was the greatest of Sam's long career,
and he gave it top priority.
For it would earn him seven million bucks,
and help advance the cause of ducks,
who still, in prime time news,
were a minority.

THE COUNTDOWN AND THE BLAST-OFF

The young Astronomer,
pleased that everyone
had boarded in a timely way,
asked the Delegation
to assemble in a forward bay.
Said he, The countdown has begun.
I would suggest that anyone
who needs to use the pot,

should run right now and do it.

The Shrink, a venerable wheeze
(who had already cut the cheese,
and everybody knew it),
decided he had better go,
but stayed so long upon the throne
(not having yet resolved
his problem with retention),
that as the minutes ticked away
all felt some apprehension.

With only fourteen seconds
on the clock when finally
the john was free,
McDonalduck stood up. Shrugged he,
I'm going in there anyway.
A Duck who makes
twelve million bucks a year
(and seven million to be here),
should feel quite free to pee
whenever he might want to pee.
They certainly
will hold the countdown till I'm done.
Alas, no sooner had he climbed up,
squatted, and begun,
there came a mighty blast.
It wasn't something Sam had passed.
It was the space ship lifting off so fast
the Duck was pressed against the pot.

Oh, well, he still could see,
as off they went,
God's stellar panoply
through that small porthole by the vent.
Indeed, just minutes into flight
McDonalduck could plainly see,
as none before him ever had,

the earth and other planets
rotating around the sun.
Around the *sun*? Egad!
What a surprise!
Then there was no sun*set* or *rise*?
Is this a scoop or *what?*

It clearly was the biggest story
man or duck had ever nailed
since whatsisname had sailed
from Spain and found
the earth was round.
Then, reaching for his micro-cam,
he realized...*damn*,
he'd left the film behind!
Thought Sam, Well, never mind,
I'm not yet dead,
I'll use the mobile phone instead.
So with the cell phone hid
beneath his feathery toupee,
Sam sent the word direct to CBA:
EARTH ROTATES AROUND SUN!

And by the time
the gravities that pressed on him
had dropped from ten to none,
and he had pooped and pooped again
and pulled the chain to flush it on its way,
his scoop already had been flashed
around the earth,
so that in seconds everybody knew,
from TV screens and Website pages,
of that journalistic coup
that made our Sam a living legend
and a Duck for all the ages.

A WORD ABOUT...KROH

There were on Kroh one billion souls,
plus twenty-four who had
the ways and tongues of men.
Each century the number of these
'Mentians' dropped,
and it was clear that if their number
dropped again,
the Krohtians who in little ways
resembled men, would disappear.

The billion population
looked substantially alike, were plump
and covered with a yellow fluff.
In short, they were the stuff
that teddy bears are made of
and that no one
(even should they growl and huff)'s
afraid of.

The Krohtians were a simple, trusting lot,
ate manna every morning,
washed it down with dew,
and had no need for shirt or smock
or sock or shoe.
They did like sunning on a smoothish rock,
looking at the miracle
of sunlight on the sand,
and wondering about that bearded, tall,
two-legged guy who way back when
– could it have been 3000 years ago? –
arrived on Kroh.

The tall one, so it seems,
had come with friends
who were so taken with the charms

of Kroh's soft, fuzzy, female population,
they couldn't wait to plant their seed.
While this went on, the bearded stranger,
who appeared to lack that need
(preferring, for himself, self-flagellation),
performed some magic tricks
and lectured long and well.
Though what he talked about
no one could tell. They simply
couldn't understand his tongue,
not even words like 'God' and 'Son'.

And then one day the stranger died.
At the time, some Krohtians half suspected
he'd been crucified and resurrected.
But, whatever had occurred,
they all now did agree
that since the stranger came to call
Kroh hadn't been the same at all.

THE GALLEY

The larders, shelves,
and freezers of the ship
were liberally stocked with things to eat
for humans, ducks and crocs.
Behind the pantry locks
were veggies, fruit, live crabs,
and *cuisses de* frog,
five different breeds of frozen dog,
whole zebra loins and tails of ox
to tempt the fussiest of crocs.

To keep their food, their drink and snacks

from floating freely in the air,
they ate and drank from plastic sacks
and space bowls made of Tupperware.

Each morn they ended nightly fasts
with eggs from laying hens,
at noon drank wine with steak or roast,
at night had caviar on toast.

To feed the Duck,
a dozen bags of unpopped corn
were stowed on board.
Of course, McDonalduck did rightly scorn
– said he *abhorred* – such rustic fare,
preferred black caviar and Scottish hare.
Still, Velcroed in his bed at night,
in secrecy, with appetite,
the Duck did pour those kernels down,
remembering, with smile and frown,
the hardships, trials – and distant charm –
of ducklinghood on master's farm.

EN ROUTE

The first day of the flight was great,
but after that, all stars began to look alike.
They saw the Dippers
and Orion's Belt disintegrate
within a void of black.
Then all the constellations of the Zodiac
did come undone,
and even the Astronomer
could not determine which was star
and which was sun.

Although the food
(donated by a company desiring publicity)
at first kept spirits high,
the travelers began to fear
the only trait they all did share
was *being* there.
And so a dreary disconnection
spread throughout the group,
with one exception: Sam McDonalduck.

Said he, If we take turns and tell the tales
of who we are and why we've come,
we could work through this tedium.

The idea pleased them, but alas,
the first to volunteer
was that one horse's ass
they *didn't* want to hear,
the right-wing Politician, Michael Jones,
whose stated mission was to broaden
his name recognition.

Asked several of the Delegation,
Man, isn't there some *other* thing
that you could do,
like go up front and bore the crew?

And so Mike went,
but found the crew already bored,
and so it wasn't time well spent.

THE PHILOSOPHER

When Mike had left,
Philosopher Bill James stood up.
He was a man of average mien,
his hair was combed,
his glance was keen.
He wore a suit of grey,
and with his power tie
(red dots upon a field of yellow),
looked the very model
of a corporate goodfellow.

Said he, I'm working for a company
that exports Beauty, Happiness, and Truth.
It's called Pragmatics, Inc.
We're paid to think,
but not to endlessly engage
in metaphysical dispute
on every sort of absolute.
No, no, we deal in action and results.
And then, to make sure these
do perfectly combine,
we test our theories on the bottom line.

I think that what you mean,
spoke up the CEO,
is that, if Truth be told,
there's nothing on the earth
more Beautiful than gold,
and Happiness begins
when profits rise tenfold.

That's Pragmatism in a nutshell
nodded James,
a system of philosophy
American as apple pie.

We do not waste our time discussing Ethics,
where our clients go to when they die,
or if they wise men be or fools;
we leave that to philosophers
of other schools.

Then spake the Duck:
I've heard of your Pragmatics, Inc.
You export theme parks, isn't it the truth?

As true as Truth can be,
said Billy James, agreeably.

Is not your stock at 33?

I think you're right,
unless it went up overnight.

Do you intend to sell
theme parks on Kroh?
the dedicated journalist pursued.

I do not know, and if I did I would not say.
For though we're far away,
afloat in space and time,
insider trading's still a crime.

I'll cut you in,
Sam whispered in his ear.

In that case, yes, the pragmatist replied.
We hope to sell them three or four a year.
But don't forget, you didn't hear it here.

I've gotta go, said Sam to all the rest.
I'll be right back. Then, when alone,
Sam opened up his mobile phone
and to his broker back on earth did say,

Al, buy 5000 Prag today.
And then he called up CBA
to break the scoop about a deal
Pragmatics, Inc. had closed,
to sell each year
a dozen theme parks to the Krohs
for some ten-figure sum they'd not disclose.

Then Sam returned
to where the others waited,
tossed back a plastic sack of brew,
and no one knew
the coup
he celebrated.

THE CROCS

It was clear to all on board
that there were two
(besides, perhaps, the crew)
who hated being there.
These were the Crocodiles,
such shy and gentle quadrupeds
that all believed them newlyweds.

Alas, not so,
for when McDonalduck, to break the ice,
began to delve into their facts of life,
he quickly learned
that they were not a Croc and wife.

We met last Tuesday, said the male,
whose name was Lash,
on that long-running show *The Mating Game*.
In case you don't already know,

the format goes like so:
A female has to choose a mate
between three bachelors,
and her selection's based upon replies
to several questions
that she poses to the guys.

What kind of questions, asked the Duck?

Oh, good ones, said young Lash.
Like, if I came to take her on a date,
and her dad opened up the door,
and when I shook his foot (or hand or paw)
it fell right off, what would I do?

Good question, nodded Sam,
and wrote it down. And so
your answers won her heart?

Not really, blushed Ms. Cocadile,
but Lash, you see, appeared to be
the only *croc* among the three.
The other two were men,
one white, one not.
Well, call me stupid, call me square,
I felt I didn't dare throw in my lot
with anyone outside my genus,
just in case there was no place
to interface between us.

You ought to be ashamed, said Sam,
who saw the headline forming in his brain:
BIGOTRY ON *MATING GAME!*
SHE SPURNS BLACK FOR ONE OF OWN.
So how did you and whatsisname
get way up here?

Well, Lash and I had never flown.

We thought our prize might be
a limo ride to Disney World
or some such other happy place.
Instead, they hurled us into outer space,
all Velcroed underneath from snout to tail.
We're terrified that should Lash
hug me to his heart,
we might never pull apart.

The startling image
that her fears had wrought,
gave them all some food for thought.

MEANWHILE, UP ON KROH...

The imminent arrival of a space ship
thrilled the Krohtians.
Rocks and pebbles lying motionless
for decades, now were picked up, dusted,
turned around, and readjusted
into patterns pleasing to the eye.

Speculation on the nature
of the Earthling mission
dominated contemplation –
what the strangers walked like,
ate and drank, were they smooth or haired,
even what diseases they might bring.
Not that anybody cared.
For Kroh had friendly germs
that guarded them both day and night.
Some grew as large as pit bulls,
growled, were full of fight,
whereas others were so small
they hardly seemed like germs at all.

The 24-strong Mentian population,
expecting to engage their guests
in social conversation,
devoted one entire week
to polishing their Earthspeak,
reading scriptures,
practicing badminton and croquet
and, in short, in every way,
prepared themselves for Landing Day.

THE BIO-PROSPECTOR

While everybody knew what a General,
a Rabbi, and a Navajo were for,
all were curious about the Bio-Prospector,
and urged that Delegate to take the floor.

Ned Bunter was a man with rugged face,
was short and thin,
a fellow who could easily fit in
the smallest space.
And that's felicitous, said he,
for one who wants to be
a microbe hunter, which is what I am.

What kind of microbes
do you hunt? asked Sam.
And why and where?

We hunt them, Bunter said,
at temperature extremes,
inside of glaciers, in volcanic rock
beneath the ice that teems
with microscopic life.

It's there we find extremophiles so old,
so focused and expedient,
that Time itself becomes
their primary ingredient.

We hunt them too
in nuclear reactor cores.
We go in submarines
down to the ocean floors
where thermal chimneys from
the earth's hot core
raise water temps to
three hundred degrees and more.

Observed the Duck,
To me, it seems impossible
that life can live in such extremes.

But, Ned replied, remember, Sam,
that when the earth began
it was a boiling sea.
All sorts of life was born of this,
including man.
Some calculate that Eden must have been
as hot as Hades;
that the DNA of Adam
must have burned like hot macadam
when he visited the ladies.
(I refer, of course, to Lilith and to Eve,
in which so many good Americans believe.)

Sam scratched his pate, then asked, confused,
For what the devil are these microbes *used*?

For making medicines, said Bunter,
and detergents too.
I bio-prospect for a firm called Sudsless, Inc.
whose products help you wash your clothes

at lower temps in tub or sink.
And Sam, I have a hunch that up on Kroh
I'll find a bunch of local germs containing
enzymes of a type to get Kroh's x-teen billion
shirts and socks and shorts a dazzling white
in water cold as cold (which as you know
could save those Krohtians quite a lot
when measured by the kilowatt).
And then, when I get home,
I'll spend my bonus on a yacht.

Said Sam, I've heard
good things of Sudsless, Inc.
Their stock's at 51, I think.

Yessir, said Ned, you could be right,
unless it went up overnight.

McDonalduck then told the rest to carry on,
while he went off to use the pho...uh...john.

THE REVEREND AND THE RABBI

The hours sped
as on through space they flew.
To be well-entertained and fed
is what most voyagers aspire to,
so these were quite content.

The morning of day four,
Evangelist Tom Beal
and Rabbi Becky Schwister took the floor.
They had been asked to get up side by side,
were given strict time limits,
and told to speak in alternating minutes.

Why all these rules?
The Delegation members were no fools.
All said they'd rather be lobotomized or dead
instead of what they most abhorred:
captive, proselytized and bored.

And too, since everybody knew
that Jew and Christian
(following a long tradition)
viewed each other with suspicion,
more as rivals than as sister or as brother,
all felt it would be much more fun
to watch one going at the other.

Beal, of whom they all had heard,
arose, and quickly gave his word
that *he'd* not try to stretch his time.
Indeed, all knew the last 'time'
that he'd opted not to 'stretch'
was not in minutes, but in years –
a stretch he'd served
with other racketeers
inside a jail. For Beal,
despite his virtuous convictions
and divine connections,
had been convicted
of the spending of donations
from his vast, adoring, TV congregation,
not on good works, charity and such,
but on a mansion down in Texas,
and a mistress and a Lexus.

Even Lash and Coca knew
that Beal's TV career was through.
That he, an object of derision,
had been banned from raising funds
or praising God on television.

But, said Beal,
the Savior has forgiven me.
Last month He gave a sign
that I should be an inter-global missionary,
told me I should fly to Kroh
and let those heathens know
that if they truly will believe
that He did come from high above
with truth and love,
and died atoning for their sins,
and if they will obey God's laws
to honor father, mother, sister, wife,
and give donations to our Cause,
they will receive eternal life.

So saying, Reverend Beal did send
a smile of triumph toward
the Rabbi, Becky Schwister,
as if to say, Top that one, sister.

But Sam McDonalduck could not resist
to jump right in as journalist
and ask Tom Beal,
Did He upon the cross atone
for Krohtian sins as well?

Of course, Beal easily replied.
I'm sure that if you dig into the history of Kroh,
you'll find a kind of parallel.
You'll find an apple and a tree,
a woman, man and serpent too,
you'll find a sin, a fall from grace,
a need to save the Krohtian race.
And since Christ can't be everywhere at once,
or die in agony a thousand times
upon a thousand crosses,
clearly He preferred to cut His losses,
die just once for half Jerusalem to see,

then leave it up to Matt and Luke
and guys like me, to spread the word
throughout the universe and history.

I see, responded Sam, and made a note.
And now it's Rabbi Schwister's turn.

Said she, I recently did learn
that there may be on Kroh
a group called Mensch
or, in the plural, Menschen.
As some of you may know,
in German and in Yiddish
this word means human being.
It is my theory that these Menschen
are diasporatic Jews,
perhaps descendants of Hebrews
who in a kind of mass ascension
went to Kroh as many as
three thousand years ago,
though how or why I do not know.
It could have been to flee
some feudal intervention,
like a pogrom or an inquisition.

Anyway, it's my intention
and my mission,
wheresoe'er my people roam,
on land or sea or Kroh or foam,
to find them all and bring them home.

So saying, Rabbi Schwister raised her chin
and flung a glance at Reverend Beal
as if to say, Your turn, schlemiel.

McDonaldduck was so impressed
by these displays of piety and erudition,
he blurted out the sad admission

that the Bible was a book he'd never read.
It seems that as a duckling,
Sam had found it easier
to spread upon the ground and read
a quarterly called *Plough & Seed*.
This fascinating tract inspired Sam,
a duck who only swam and quacked,
to seek another form of self-expression,
and led him to the news profession.

But who can tell?
Perhaps, had he back then
the opportunity to read God's word,
he might well have preferred
to lead a congregation,
and become the richest pulpiteer
on any network TV station.

I've heard, said Sam,
that God created man.
But did he also create ducks?
For that is what I am.

Of course, replied the Rabbi.
Let me see. If ducks are birds,
I think he made them on day five.
But if they are domesticates,
like cows and dogs and chicks,
he probably created them,
along with men and crocodiles,
the next day, which was six.

Sam turned to Reverend Beal.
Do ducks have souls? he asked.
And if so, are there men like you
or ducks somewhere, who
spread the word
that true-believing waterfowl

can go to heaven too?

These were questions neither Beal
nor Schwister'd ever heard.
It being lunch time, he demurred
to answer them without
a great deal more reflection.
Meanwhile, he concurred
with her suggestion
that after lunch the floor should go
to the Psychiatrist, the Poet
or the Navajo.

THE PSYCHIATRIST

The midday meal was great,
but after each had licked his plate
(or spoon, or bill),
and had together drained
two kegs of brew on tap,
they all were dying for a nap.
And so they voted
to wake up again at four,
at which time Dr. Harry Fink,
the shrink, would take the floor.

The hours passed.
When all had ceased to snore,
up stood the wheeze.
I couldn't help but note, said he
(in accents noticeably Viennese),
that when it comes to matters of religion,
there often seems
some competition, or division,
between the Christians and the Jews.

I think this is because Christ is perceived
to be the Son of God.

Now, happy as a father/son
relationship can be,
there may occur
(no matter if the birth is virgin),
eine kleine jealousy,
what Freud has called
ein Komplex Oedipal.
I cannot think that Jesus took it well
to be forsaken on a cross.
Was this his father's way
of showing who was boss?
If so, it didn't work.

The story goes,
that from his tomb the son arose
and flew to heaven's highest throne
to head a new religion of his own.
For this he stole his father's title, God.
And then, as often is the case,
the son not only did replace
but did outpace his pa,
attracting possibly, by now,
two billion true believers.
And of this number quite a few
did persecute the Jew,
crusaded against Muslims too,
and colonized the Hindu.

When Fink was through,
they all looked blank.
Not one had ever heard
a summing up so frank.
Was this Psychiatrist
some sort of crank?

The only one to speak was Lash.
Said he, I never knew my reptile dad.
A foster home is all I had.
But if I ever find the man who had the gall
to kidnap me when I was small,
I'll fight him, and defeat him,
and when he's drowned I'll eat him.

On hearing this, the shrink did muse,
I never had a son myself,
but once, in YO, I found
a little croc upon the ground
and took it home and raised it like a son.
But when the crocodile
grew large enough to challenge me
with tooth and guile,
I thought on Oedipus awhile,
and when there came a heavy rain,
I pushed it down a sewer drain.
The doctor sighed.
Said he, I hope you see
that even a Psychiatrist like me,
can be a victim of psychology.

As Dr. Fink made his admission,
a look of recognition
filled the young Croc's eyes.
Alas, as he was starting to arise
and take a step, Lash caught
his Velcroed tail and chin
upon the carpeting,
and to his terrible chagrin
got stuck fast in the middle of the floor.
Then, seeing his beloved Coca smile,
the awkward Crocodile
just shut his eyes, scrunched down,
and moved no more.

So why, Sam asked the shrink,
are you en route to Kroh?
Are you researching something
that the rest of us should know?

I have a theory, answered Fink. I think,
from evidence I have amassed,
the Krohtian ego may have crashed
as long as thirty centuries ago,
though how or why I do not know.
But it is *klar*
from what we have observed so far
(concerning lack of team sports,
smokestack factories, and such),
that Krohtians are completely out of touch
with any sort of competition.

What I would like to learn
is what a creature *thinks* all day,
without ambition
or the stresses and distractions
of stock markets, politics, and war,
of sports, illicit sex,
and every other need and yen
that aggravate
our three-score years and ten.

I don't know why, but I suspect
that you, my friends, and I,
would simply *die*
without our daily dose of television,
shows that terrify us, make us laugh or cry,
or make us seethe
with feelings of deep loathing and derision.
I know that when I watch the nightly news,
and see you, dear McDonalduck,
pontificate, insinuate,
express your shallow views,

I feel the pressure of my blood rise up
until I almost lose my mind!
And yet I find, and do admit,
I am so hooked, that every day
I turn the knob to CBA
and risk an apoplectic fit.

McDonalduck was pleased
by what he'd heard.
I do my best, he modestly averred,
to make my listeners return for more.
They do not pay a Duck
twelve million bucks a year to be a bore.
And if you want to know,
my mission is to pave the way for CBA
to that huge market up on Kroh.

A GENERAL DISCUSSION

(Including the Real Estate Developer,
the Cartographer, the Geologist,
the Economist, and the Duck.)

Thanks to their frank debates,
the ice had broken.
The Delegates agreed
that those who'd spoken
had done well.
But now their space ship
was approaching Kroh,
the tension growing,
and all felt it was the time
for some to ask informally
what they most wished to know.

I wish to know,
said Real Estate Developer
Ms. Tessie Rubble,
as she adjusted her blue blazer,
whether Kroh has cities, suburbs,
coastlines, hills and lakes.
And if she has, by just what standards
should an Earth person appraise her?
Admittedly, I should have researched this
before I came, but at the time
was being driven half insane
by a lawsuit down in Texas:
'Wetlands vs Multiplexes'.
The odds against us everybody thought
were ten to none,
but, praise the Lord, we won.

On hearing this, another traveler joined in.
My name, said he, is Jack Perone.
My specialty is that branch of cartography
that deals with planets other than our own.
I'm glad to tell Ms. Rubble
that not very long ago,
a space ship carrying a Hubble
photographed the planet Kroh.
She does have cities, six in all,
with buildings tens of meters tall.
There were no highways to be found,
which indicates that Krohtians have the skill
to put mass transit underground.

Then he went on,
The planet has four continents,
three oceans and a hill.
Even with ecologists to litigate each sale,
a charming alien like you
would certainly prevail.

All chuckled as Ms. Rubble blushed,
and then the room got hushed
to hear another Delegate.

His face was weathered, his suit tweedy,
his leather elbow patches genteelly seedy.
His dark blue shirt was polyester drip-dry,
and around his collar
was a skinny, beaded, string tie.

Said he, my name is Steven Clift,
and I'm the chief Geologist
at Continental Plate & Drift,
a firm who's name and logo
you are surely all familiar with.
My special disciplines are mineralogy,
petrology, and groundwater geology.
And I am sure you folks already know,
or have an educated guess,
what I'll be doing up on Kroh.

While Clift was speaking, Sam was in a state.
He owned a thousand shares
of Continental Plate.
Should he buy more before it was too late?

So, said the Duck, will you inform us
if you find some pricey ore,
or will we have to suffer through a wait eternal,
and read it in *The Wall Street Journal?*

At this, up spoke Economist Ben Carter.
Before, said he, we start to dream
of profit and of gain,
before we scrutinize each inch of Kroh's terrain
and measure, weigh and chart her,
we have to ascertain
that Krohtians have hard currencies,

and do not deal in sea shells, scrip, or barter.

For all *we* know, the planet Kroh
could be a globe of solid gold.
Of course, should this be so,
following Sam's urgent news flash
Earth's economy might crash.
The first catastrophe would be
when ingots piled up in Fort Knox,
in Krugerland, and underneath Red Square
became as valueless as rocks.
A thing is precious only when it's rare.

On hearing this, McDonalduck,
defying lack of gravity, leaped on a chair.
We journalists believe
that people have a right to know,
and it's our duty to bring everything to light.
Like, did the president
approve the burglary that night,
trade arms for hostages,
or have a love affair?
A journalist will proudly air
the least substantiated rumors.
Yet, had *I* to make the call
on whether to announce to all
that Kroh is made of gold,
and risk the possibility
that Earth's economy would fold,
I swear, this Duck would hold his quack.
So put away your fears.
At *most*, he'd take some pebbles back
as souvenirs.

THE POET AND THE CEO

When Sam was done,
a thin, morose, young man
named Terry Wright, a Poet,
who'd never eaten half so well
in all his life as on this trip
(although his manner didn't show it),
coughed, to indicate
that he had something to relate.

But when the others looked at him,
they saw with some dismay
that his white shirt was grey
and that his cuffs showed fray.
Why was he on the ship?
Because the young Astronomer,
whose name was Rip,
had wanted it that way.

I'm off to Kroh, said Wright,
but not on some evangelizing mission,
or to reap a monetary gain.
No, my reason's plain.
I'm simply tired of the Earth.
Little do I see in nature that is worth
what it was worth the moment of my birth.
I've lived but one-score years,
and yet I know where're I go
that there have passed away
a thousand glories from the earth.

Unlike our uncle, Wordsworth,
did *my* generation come
trailing clouds of smoke
from hell, which is our womb.
And so I'm on my way to Kroh
to find a better world, or find a tomb.

At this, up spoke the CEO,
whose name was Arnold Robb.
Said he, I have a son called Bob
who is, like you, just one-score...wait...
I think...oh, hell, I'd have to say
the kid is one-score years and *three*
if he's a day.
Bob owns a Harley and an SUV,
and you can bet I've never heard *him* whine.
He doesn't lie around and pine
for what he thinks he cannot get.
He spends his time
at futures trading on the Internet.
My boy, you should be more like Bob;
get on the Net or find a job.

And then he laughed.
Perhaps you've never noticed
the condition of your pants and shirt.
Or do you fear dry cleaning them
would set off an ozone alert?

Replied the youth,
A wise man gave me some advice.
He was a banker by profession.
I met him at a time when
I was under the impression
I could get a bank loan
and thus better my condition.
But my collateral was text.

The man did not show me the door
or tell his secretary
whom to send in next.
He carefully explained to me
if there be rich there must be poor,
just like, if there be hot there must be cold,

if peace, then war, if bought, then sold.

So, though he turned down my appeal,
I didn't feel he'd given me the boot.
He made me see
a man can serve a social purpose
higher than his poesy,
just by being destitute.
I felt he really gave a hoot.

And then this banker turned,
picked up his ringing phone,
and maybe just to prove to me
his absolute consistency
and strict impartiality,
he gave a guy he'd never met
a million-dollar loan.

The Poet smiled.
Who knows, old boy, he told the CEO.
Perhaps when this strange trip is done,
by which time I'll be twenty-one,
I'll go back home and follow your advice.
I'll sacrifice my melancholy and my theme,
I'll put aside my dream
of meadow, grove and stream
apparelled in celestial light.
And then, like you and sonny,
I'll occupy myself with money –
learn where money comes from,
where it goes,
why it stagnates,
where it flows,
why devalues,
how it grows.
And once I know,
I'll write a story about money
using *New York Times* official prose,

or find some even drier way to tell it.
And then I'll hold my nose
and try to sell it.

When Terry Wright was done,
it wasn't clear
if he'd been serious or cavalier.
Before one Delegate
could think of what to say,
word came that caviar
was being served up in the dining bay.
Not because the Poet was a bore
was everyone so keen to dash;
they simply wished to eat some more.
But there...oh dear!...was Lash,
still Velcroed to the floor.

A member of the crew was called
to undo the disaster.
He grabbed the poor Croc by the tail
and faster than the eye could see
gave one quick tug
that ripped Lash off the rug
like an adhesive plaster.
Without a pause the crewman flipped him,
stripped him of the band of Velcro
lining him from snout to tush,
gave the Croc a little push,
at which, to everyone's relief,
Lash floated toward his Cocadile
who reached out with a loving smile
and drew him near.

And there the two Crocs clung and kissed,
and never knew what meals they missed.

THE GENERAL AND THE NAVAJO

The General looked trim and smart.
Her skirt came just below the knees,
and on her heart,
instead of brooches, bows
and other female ostentations,
stood three sober rows
of military decorations.

Said she, whose name was Dora Battle,
I don't engage in idle prattle.
The purpose of my trip
is classified top secret
and I don't intend to leak it.
But, before you all begin
to enter in wild speculation
on why I and my assistant,
Private Rabbit Stalker,
are aboard this ship,
you ought to know
that there is precedent
for meaningful collaboration
between General and Navajo.

In the year of '42,
the United States Marines
inducted and instructed
hundreds of brave Navajos
on how to transmit military data
on field radios.
Rabbit's granddad, Coyote Stalker,
was a Navajo 'Code Talker'.
Their native tongue was so obscure
the Japs could not translate it,
much less stop it.
So why are we en route to Kroh?

You'll never know,
and so, just drop it.

When the General sat down,
McDonalduck stood up.
His heart was full.
Military secrets were to him
just so much bull.
Any journalist could see
that all the stuff
on Navajos in World War II
was just a bluff,
a mist, a clever ploy
to hide a taxpayer-paid tryst
between an officer and boy.

And so he said, I cannot think
what secret, nowadays, an Indian
and General could share.
The Earth, that one calls mother,
is exactly what the other
seeks to blow into the air
or overlay with surplus junk.
And yet, since opposites attract
– or so they say –
one thing a General and Navajo
might share today
would be a bunk.

At this the private turned so pale,
the General did blush so bright,
it wasn't clear which was the Redskin,
which the White.

You've gone too far!
exclaimed the Delegation.
Even you, a Duck,
should know you've sullied both the army

and a noble Indian nation.
How dare a Duck infer that Private Stalker
is the General's own 'pillow talker'?

Shrugged the journalist,
Inference is proof enough.
I'll bet my reputation CBA will air this stuff
and give me thanks.
Sexual harassment in the ranks
our viewers find most titillating.
It drives up our Nielsen rating.

Heaven help us, sighed the wheeze,
for now we're privileged to know
the TV sleaze we'll find awaiting
when we all return from Kroh.

THE POLITICIANS

The entire Delegation,
anticipating speeches from the Politicians
(one black, one white, one left, one right,
both seeking the same seat,
and both – Oh, save us, Lord! –
named Michael Jones),
were so darn sure that they'd be
traumatized or bored,
they wished the pols
would simply die or go away.

And so it was with real dismay
they heard the journalist Duck say
that he looked forward to Election Day
and all the months along the way.

I understand you're on this trip,
said he to Michael Jones (the White),
to strengthen your name recognition.
If this is right,
I wonder how you'll reach that aim
without it strengthening the same
belonging to the opposition.

That crossed my mind, said Jones,
and my position on it is,
as soon as I return from Kroh
I'll change my moniker to Dwight
in honor of that General
who back in 1952
won *his* big presidential fight.
And then I'll run with
his great slogan, 'I Like Dwight'.

I think, frowned Sam McDonalduck,
you're making a mistake.
If *both* of you are Michael Jones,
I'll have a hook for interviews and other stuff,
enough to make your name well known.
I couldn't care less which one wins,
but in this polarizing game
your name would look as cute as twins.

Hey, guys, cut in the blacker Politician,
everything is cool. If my right-wing opponent
wants to change his name to Dwight,
I'll run my race on 'I Like Mike'.
For any fool can see that 'Mike', like 'Ike',
rhymes better with 'I like' than 'Dwight'.

You *wouldn't*, cried the whiter Mike
who felt his throat was growing tight.
I thought that 'I Wike Dight' was wight,
but now I see it's vewy wong.

My whole campaign will wun amok
unless I do wike blacker Mike
and make my slogan 'I Like Duck'.

Then do it, said the journalist,
and don't lose heart.
A space trip's great to jump-start
your political careers.
Just look at Senator John Glenn.
He's been up twice.
Should he decide to run again
he'd surely win, though he by then
be old as four-score years and ten.
But in your case
a single trip to outer space
should help you both on voting day
which is but twenty months away.

That's right,
sighed Michael Jones, the White.
The time remaining's getting tight.
Campaigning is no piece of cake.
I haven't yet begun fund-raising,
much less finalized the phrasing
of the promises I'll break...uh, make.

Don't worry, said McDonalduck.
If you have pluck, are dedicated, tough,
and demonstrate a little cunning,
twenty months is time enough
to figure out why you are running.

THE LAST SUPPER

It was the final evening of the trip.
To calm whatever apprehensions
might grip passengers and crew,
a simple meal had been prepared –
a spicy meat-potato whip
delicious on a nacho chip.

Later, over cognac, Rip,
the young Astronomer, said,
Folks, whatever lies ahead,
remember that we come in peace
to foster inter-global trade,
not to pillage, con or fleece.
Whatever private aim or vain ambition
some of us have brought along,
it must be junior to our mission.

We know not what we'll find on Kroh,
what kind of people, customs,
ways of thought, but we have brought
good food to eat and other stuff
to last at least a week or two,
and that should give us time enough
to do what we will seek to do.

Now get some rest and don't feel worried;
we've been blessed with one fine crew.

And so the Delegation hurried off to bed.
And though some winked at one another,
not a further word was said.

THE VIGIL

Not so long ago from now
a Landing Day was nigh.
A billion pairs of Krohtian eyes
were fixed, in different azimuths,
upon the Krohtian sky.
Krohtian newborns, who grew fast,
arriving in a week or two at their full size,
intuitively knew
the first thing that they wished to do
was spot that space ship in the blue.

No prize was offered for the first to sight it.
Even so, they watched and waited,
and in their quiet Krohtian way,
for reasons that they could not say,
all felt elated.

PART TWO:

KROH

THE ARRIVAL

Next morning on awakening,
the Delegation found their ship
already on the ground.
Outside its panoramic windows
lay a wide, flat land,
graced into infinity
with rocks and pebbles
placed upon the sand
in patterns pleasing to the eye.
In the distance,
sudden as a bunch of flowers,
bloomed a dozen slender towers.

Everywhere on this great vista,
showing leisurely persistence,
creatures bent on their subsistence
chipped white wafers off the rocks,
washed them down with dew,
and, despite a keen elation
triggered by a space ship
lying silently within their view,
kept on gathering their ration
as each morning Krohtians do.

Toward ten o'clock, a small committee
numbering some twenty-four,
taller than the other billion,
waited by the spaceship door.
There they stood most patiently
until the Earthlings inside finished
yawning, stretching, stripping Velcro
from their feet or tail or legs,
washed and dressed,
and with a certain zest diminished
stacks of pancakes, fries and eggs.

When done, and ready for what was to come,
the Delegation stood beside their leader, Rip,
and watched the front door of the ship
swing wide,
revealing them to all outside.

We come to Kroh in peace,
said the Astronomer, and led them out
into an atmosphere so fresh,
a day so clear and soft,
that if it had occurred on Earth,
total strangers in the street
would have doffed their isolation,
bowed, and asked each other, Brother,
sister, have you ever breathed
an air so sweet?

Filled with philosophic pleasure,
Billy James removed his tie.
Said he, I feel like I could fly.
This breeze is neither cool nor warm,
but lies exactly in between,
an absolute and golden mean.
If Kroh is like this every day
and if this landscape is the norm,
then with uncompromising rigor
I will certainly re-figure,
make the target number bigger,
of the quantity of theme parks
(which you know I won't disclose)
that Pragmatics, Inc. proposes
selling yearly to the Krohs.

Then said one Krohtian elder
to the visitors from space,
Welcome to our planet.
Proper nouns are never used by us,
but if it's easier for you

to call a thing by name,
we'll make no fuss
and happily will play your game.
We'll call our planet Kroh,
and I'll be Ken, and that is Rex,
and over there is Moe.

Then he went on, And one thing more,
we do appreciate your greeting,
but it's meaningless to say
you come to Kroh in peace, for,
if there is peace there must be war,
and war is something Kroh has not.
We also have no cold or hot,
no bought or sold.
Indeed, we have no money and no gold,
which means, therefore,
that we've no rich and we've no poor.

Meanwhile, the Duck was taking notes.
Said Sam, We called your planet Kroh
when your distaste for proper names
we did not know.
Nor could we *a priori* guess
that Krohtians feel a lot of stress
with to and fro and more and less.
When we arrived, I clearly see,
Rip should have just said, 'Here we be'.

Good try, said Ken, but no cigar.
I hate to sound particular,
but it is clear that *here* implies
that there's a *there*,
to *be* has got a *not* to be,
and *we,* you must admit, has *they*.

Then what, asked Sam,
should new arrivals like us say?

It doesn't matter, answered Moe.
Just use whatever words you know.
We only wanted you to see
that proper nouns and opposites
are not in our philosophy.
We are exactly what we are,
no special names or set extremes.
We think that it's in language
where the danger of partition lies.
All creatures would live
happily together otherwise.

I fink, said Michael Jones, the White,
whose throat again was growing tight,
that your philosophy is wong.
That Michael Jones is black and weft,
not rite and extreme-wight like me.
If we could not chase after votes
with speeches, threats and anecdotes
describing all our diffwences,
how could any constituency
choose between that Jones and me?
I say, to wid the world of 'us' and 'them',
and even 'him' and 'it' and 'she',
would be a kind of twavesty
that would destroy Democwacy.

As for the take you have on names,
it's tough enough that both of us
are Michael Jones,
but he and I would wook like *cwowns*
if someone outlawed proper nouns.
I have to say, in closing, it is *bitchin'*,
having come so far to stwengthen
my name wecognition,
to land where names,
(and pwobably political ambition)

are wooked upon with wank suspicion.

I think, said Moe, we should come clean.
It's easy for us here to act
linguistically pristine,
when, actually, in point of fact,
just twenty-four of us have tongues
while there's a billion who are dumb.
We few who can, do rarely speak
and normally keep very mum,
except on special Landing Days
when folk from other planets come.

Well, I am sure, said Dr. Fink,
that Krohs do have *some* opposites
like females and like males.
And furthermore, I do suspect
that on your planet there are times
when calling heads or tails
with quarters, nickels, even dimes
is perfectly correct.

I ought to tell you folks, said Rex,
we Krohtians have but just one sex,
in such a way that moms are dads.

Wait, Rex, said Ken, our scriptures say....

But Rex went on,
This works, it's clear,
because we have no rednecks here
to beat us up or call us queer.
And as for tossing heads or tails,
this would require coins that flip.
Since Kroh does not have currency,
not even scrip,
our former argument prevails.

At this, Economist Ben Carter
pulled a string of beads
from his vest pocket, beads
in colors never seen before on Kroh.
The colors made their eyes grow wide
and several laughed while others sighed.
It wasn't joy, it wasn't rue,
in fact, the opposite was true;
it simply was what Krohtians do
when seeing beads of unknown hue.

Okay, said Ben,
let's try that greeting once again:
We come to Kroh with beads.

And then he held the beads toward Ken
who said, You're onto something, Ben.
And Ken then took the proffered strand,
examined it, and frowned, and said,
Beads talk more pointedly than men.
For these I'll give you rocks and sand,
what some call 'undeveloped land'.
And then he grinned and said to Carter,
I think we just invented barter.

BONDING

The morning passed in idle chat
between the Delegation
and their Krohtian hosts.
That afternoon a picnic lunch
was served outside the ship,
and there the Delegates made toasts
with beer and wine and lemonade
to future inter-global trade.

The Krohs, who normally drank only dew,
were finally prevailed upon
to try an ice cold glass of brew.
Alas, the alcohol went to their heads
and to their great dismay
they lost at badminton and even at croquet,
batting shuttlecocks to earth,
smacking balls so hard they flew,
and when a friendly germ
was accidently put in play,
the germ got smacked and batted too.

After things calmed down a little,
Rabbi Schwister turned to Moe.
I'd really like to know, said she,
if you and Ken and all your friends
are of some special race.
You're taller than the billion,
speak like men, and have
a certain something in your face
that shows, despite your non-dualistic pose,
an inner angst or tension
and a somewhat largish nose.
Could you possibly be Menschen?

We've heard the name, said Moe.
Some say it's possible our ancestors

came here from Earth about 3000 years ago,
though how or why I do not know.
However, there exists an ancient text
that may supply a clue,
and if the rumor turns out to be true,
our great grandfathers might have looked
much less like me and Rex, than you.

I thought as much, said Rabbi Schwister,
and I'd like to ask a favor.
See Ned Bunter over there
fighting with that monster virus?
He's collecting specimens of DNA.
If you could spare some blood or hair,
it could apprise us
who you are and where you're from.

Tell Bunter he can come, said Moe,
and I'll be waiting.
And tell him not to mind
if he should find me
cowering and hyper-ventilating.
Meanwhile, if you'd like to see that book....

Oh, yes, said Schwister, let me take a look.
I have a feeling it could be quite devastating.

DUCK.COM

That night, as Delegation members
drifted off to find their beds,
McDonalduck was idly counting heads.

Lash and Coca still were out. It seems
that morning they had found

an old, abandoned
transportation system underground,
filled with bubbly thermal brine.
Even in their most romantic dreams,
where water turns to wine,
and in a stream of sparkling vintage
they embrace, a place more magical
could not have been divined.
And so the two had packed a lunch
and gone off to explore
its miles of track and tunnels,
hoping these might lead them
to love's farthest shore.

Who else was still awake?
Seated in the reading nook,
the Reverend and Rabbi
studied pages in a book.
Tessie Rubble and Cartographer Perone,
having gone to be alone
beneath the stars
(where she had hoped to calculate
the full cash value of the view –
or so she said),
were back inside the ship, but not in bed.

Shuddered Tessie,
brushing at her clothes and head,
slapping at her neck and face,
This place could never be a mall.
It's all a-crawl with insects,
horrid ones that race about
and leave a whitish trace
upon the rocks. Just look!
They're crawling up my socks!

Pecking one small bug off Tessie's sweater,
McDonalduck rolled up his eyes.

Not bad, said he, but there were better
on the farm when I was young.
This one was slightly bitter,
yet left a fruity aftertaste upon the tongue.

Then huffed the Real Estate Developer,
If this is what goes on at night on Kroh,
I greatly fear no way in bloody hell
will my jet-setty clientele
buy property up here.

No problem, interrupted Robb, the CEO,
a regular insomniac
out looking for a bedtime snack.
I head a firm called Surplus, Inc.
We specialize in pesticides,
the deadliest varieties
that every nation of the Earth,
spouting ecologic pieties, has banned.
I brought along a fifty-gallon drum
to sell or barter for some land.
So, if these locals don't decide to ban it,
in a week there won't be left
two insects on the planet.

Said Sam, I've heard of Surplus, Inc.
Your stock's at twenty-two, I think.

Said Robb, Last week I told my boy
that stock will soon soar out of sight,
but that is all I'll say tonight.

A moment later, as the Duck
was heading for his bunk,
he heard a snore and tripped upon
the Mentian, Ken, who'd drunk
not just one beer, but four,
and now was sleeping on the floor.

When Ken's eyes opened,
he exclaimed with philosophical delight
that it was dark and yet was light.
Said he, We Krohs begin to doze
before the sun goes down,
and soundly sleep
until it's back up in the skies.
It's just like living in Nirvana.
Each day when we arise,
we find some loving, unseen hand
has spread our manna
over rocks and sand.

Then none of you could know,
observed the Duck,
that all night long a zillion bugs appear
and ravage your poor land.

Ken shrugged. I guess we don't,
or I'd have heard.
For though our billion never speak a word,
they sign with body language,
taste, touch, sight, and sound.
Indeed, we Krohs send shrugs and hugs
the planet 'round
faster than the speed of light.
So I'd have known about the bugs.

Mused Sam, The animals on Earth
communicate with sniff and lick and spray.
I've noticed when I waddle in a certain way,
or twitch my tail, or hold my bill
at such and such a pitch,
nibble at the nib of one white quill
to stop an itch, or sneeze just so,
it never seems to mean a thing to humans,
but speaks volumes here on Kroh.

And likewise, when I see a Krohtian
move his hand or eye or head,
I understand what he has said.

Said Ken, You may be right.
But meanwhile,
just to spare myself some fright,
may I sleep in your ship tonight?

Any place is fine, said Sam,
and don't feel called upon to make reply
should you hear Crocodiles begin
their nocturnal communication.
They're making love, not conversation.

THE SMOKE SCREEN

Next morning, the entire Delegation
breakfasted outside. The General,
who'd beaten everyone at badminton
the day before,
was feeling rather stiff and sore.
At her side, in camouflage fatigues,
sat Private Rabbit Stalker,
a youth who wore the sculpted brow,
nose, lips, and cheekbones of his race
all perfectly assembled
in a cinematic face.
Despite the innuendos
that the journalist had made,
those in attendance when
she trounced him on the court
had seen there wasn't anything
between the two but sport.

The General mused to herself,
It's odd how when that Duck
went on his fishing expedition,
his obscene charges briefly made
a smoke screen for my mission.
Getting to her feet, she led
the young enlisted man aside.
Now that you've had a look at Kroh,
I want your fresh opinion
about which way we should go.

Well, sir, replied the Navajo,
I've felt some hesitation
since discovering Kroh's bleaker
than our poorest reservation.
The climate's neat,
but Indians eat meat,
and on the Krohtian plain are
only furry creatures
with cute teddy-bearish features.
And so I think we shouldn't be too hasty.
For while they look okay
for petting and for stroking,
compared to buffalo or men
they probably aren't half as tasty.
(Only joking.)

Dora Battle didn't smile as Private Stalker,
with a twinkle in his eye, went on:
We can't just push this native race aside,
or buy their sacred lands,
on which has surely splashed the blood
of brave, ancestral deeds,
with worthless strands of colored beads.
Nor does this planet seem a place
to open a casino. They have no coinage
and, what's just as inauspicious,
Krohs don't wear a stitch of clothes,

not even britches.
So, from top to toes
they have no pockets into which
a crapshooter might hope to slip
a single fifty-dollar chip.

In short, I think the army's plan
to make this planet one huge reservation,
and ship here every
squaw, brave, and papoose
of every noble Indian nation,
is bound to hit some snags.

In that case, said the General,
we'll simply plant our flags
and claim the planet for our own,
send troops,
and see to it our people are aware
we cannot tolerate a threat like Kroh
just one light week away by air.
Not to take firm action
would be looked on as remiss.
And now, because we need more smoke
to cloak our mission,
give your General a kiss.

THE OTHER CAMPSITE TALES

It was a copy of a copy
of an ancient copy
of a very old papyrus scroll
some early Krohtian
probably attempted to unroll
and saw turn into dust.
The text was writ in Hebrew,

which luckily the Rabbi knew.

These stories are as old,
she told Tom Beal, as *Genesis*.
I'd even say that they
are over forty centuries if they're a day.
I haven't read too far as yet,
but far enough to see
that whosoever wrote this down
selected different oral tales
from those we have believed to be
our mythic history.

I fear religious fundamentalists
may even think that this new take on *Genesis*
contradicts and even menaces
the deep foundations of Judeo-Christian faith.
And yet I am convinced
these tales were told at campsites
by those very tribal nomads
whom the great agnostic
and philosopher, Voltaire, did curse
as *des barbares* and worse
(although he did admit he found
the Bible readable as Homer,
so perhaps down deep he felt
'barbarian' was a misnomer).

One difference that I see
between these versions....
Oh, but wait. Give me a moment
while I find a simple story to translate.

And so the Rabbi took another look
inside the ancient holy book
and found a story she could share
with her new friend, Tom Beal, the crook.

ANOTHER GENESIS

The Lord God planted a beautiful garden in Eden. In the middle of the garden he put a pile of shekels, and said to the man and woman, "You may eat the fruit of the trees, but you may not touch those coins. If you do, you will die."

The man and the woman were both naked but they were not particularly embarrassed.

There was in the Garden a serpent who had a basket of fresh fruit. The fruit was to die for. It was more beautiful than any of the fruit on the trees, and smelled divine. The woman felt she had to eat some, but when she reached for a kumquat, the serpent told her, "The price is one shekel, fifty agorots apiece."

The woman cried, "That price is too high."

"Wrong," said the snake. "You will not find a better price in all of Eden."

"But," cried the woman, "the price is too high for someone who has no shekels and not a single agorot either."

"Wrong again," said the snake. "Look over there."

So the woman took a few shekels from the forbidden pile and gave them to the serpent. She shared the fruit with her husband. As soon as they'd eaten some, they understood what a bargain the fruit had been. They wished they knew where to get a good bargain on some animal pelts to cover their nakedness, which had begun to bother them.

When the Lord God found shekels were missing, he asked the man what had happened. The man told the Lord God that his wife had taken the money to buy fruit. "Why did you do this?" the Lord God asked the woman.

"The snake offered me a fantastic bargain," she replied.

The Lord God then told the man that for the rest of his life he would have to work hard for money, from before sunrise until the moon was high. But the more money he had, the more he would want, and the harder he would work to obtain it.

The man was appalled. "But it wasn't my fault," he told the Lord God. "The woman you gave me took the shekels. I didn't know anything about it."

The Lord God then told the woman, "You will be as greedy as the man. You will spend half your time eating, and the more you eat, the fatter you will get. The fatter you get, the more you will hate yourself. The rest of your time you will spend shopping for better and better bargains, until you drop. Shoes and childbirth will be extremely painful. If you decide to work, you will never earn as much as men do for the same labor."

Then the Lord God named the man Sneed, and the woman Tavarice [which in ancient Hebrew rhymed with greed and avarice], and made clothes for them out of animal pelts. He sewed pockets in the pants, because the Lord God knew that where there's a pocket, there's a desire to put more and more into it.

Then the Lord God told Sneed and Tavarice to go forth from Eden, find jobs, and multiply. "Having sex is good," he told them, "but the love of bargains is the root of evil."

Then the Lord God broke all the serpent's legs off and kicked him out of the Garden into the dust of the world.

THE OTHER GOSPEL

While you were studying last night,
said Beal, I took a look
inside this other Krohtian book.
And Rabbi, if you think
that tale of Tavarice and Sneed
is bound to curl some hair,
this story of the Son of God
will fill more millions with despair.

For He, you see, was here on Kroh
about three thousand years ago
with twelve disciples, all with names like
Sidney, Melvin, Josh and Steve.

Laughed Becky Schwister,
In your wildest nightmares, mister.
You expect me to believe
your Christ was up here saving souls
about ten centuries *BC*?

Sighed Beal, I know. It sounds so dumb.
And yet, a bunch of Jews did come
from ancient Palestine.
Their testament is very clear,
for four wrote down in great detail
the miracles they witnessed here.
Then at some later date,
their gospels were apparently translated
into Universal Esperanto,
cousin to a tongue I learned
when I was unjustly interned
in Corpus Christi, Texas.

We had one major problem there
that did perplex us.
The prison population

was so ethnically diverse,
the convicts babbled
every language in the universe,
from Old Sumerian to Aramaic,
New Roswellian and Greek.

We trustees, then,
to get our business done
and at the same time have a little fun,
downloaded all those languages,
hit RUN, and merged them into one
ol' user-friendly prison-speak,
not very different from the tongue
employed in his translation
by this latter-Krohtian Jesus freak.

Tom, you exaggerate, objected Schwister.
If there were old Sumerians
and Aramaeans in your jail,
I know a dozen rabbis and philologists
who gladly would have stood their bail
or bribed the guards to set them free.

What can I say? shrugged Beal,
except no scholar
ever offered fifty bucks to *me*.
Then Tom Beal shook his head and said,
These scriptures fill my soul with dread.
They show me what a glib
and facile fool I've been.
But what is worse, in chapter and in verse
they toll the knell for Christianity itself,
for heaven and for hell.

You're not convinced?
Okay, Rabbi, I know you'd rather have
a wine more kosher in your cup,
but since your mission

is to locate missing Menschen, listen up,
and listen well.
For I intend right now to read
a gospel story that reveals
the Agony of Christ our Lord
according to Apostle Mel.

But suddenly they heard a bell
announcing lunch was being served.
I'll tell you what, said Beal,
let's take a break and have our meal.
For anyway, I'm so perplexed,
I'd like to hear opinions
of some others on this text.
Although I have to say,
if we could find a way
to keep that Duck at bay,
and maybe too, the shrink,
it might be better, don't you think?

BUNTER'S AWAKENING

Ned Bunter had been working hard,
and it was clear
collecting enzymes down on Earth
was nothing like it was up here.
These germs resembled not at all
the microbes found in Arctic glaze
or in the chimneys of the sea.
Oh, no, they were extremophiles
in other ways,
like size and personality.

One monster virus,
slippery, translucent, shiny,

didn't take it kindly
when Ned tried to slip a needle
in what seemed to be its heinie.
Problem was, of course,
that germs don't have a true behind,
nor have they front, or side,
or underneath.
And while all viruses are blind,
Krohtian viruses have teeth.

Still, Bunter's intuition
told him he could beat the competition
if he'd just ignore the hurt,
and concentrate on finding
those 'designer enzymes'
that would get out Krohtian dirt
and wash each Krohtian sock and shirt
a whiter white
in water that was cold, not hot.
And in a year, when Sudsless, Inc.
had sold a billion boxes
of detergent to the Krohs,
he'd be rewarded with a yacht.

But suddenly a dawning did intrude.
He looked about and noticed...
every Krohtian was a nude!
What a *bummer*.
He'd have to use the inner tube
another summer.

Still, with enzymes off his mind,
Ned Bunter found he had the time
to do some lab work for the Rabbi.
Earlier he'd noticed
chromosomal aberrations
in the DNA already taken.

Said Bunter to himself that night,
To judge by the genetic profile
of this native population,
I'd say three thousand years ago
their forebears whiled away some time
in extra-Krohtian copulation.
For, despite the strange contention
of those four-and-twenty Menschen
that each Krohtian's both
a father and a mother,
every bit of information
I've been able to uncover
shows a lot of Krohs were fathered
by some very different other.

And so, I feel deep in my bones,
if Rabbi Schwister
follows up on her strange notion
to invite each Krohtian
who has Jewish genes
to exercise God-given rights
and emigrate to Israel
or Crown Heights, Queens,
based on her assumption
they'd be happier on Earth,
then the statistical, logistical,
political, and ecologic drama
that accompanied this move
would cause more trauma
than it's worth.

But, sighed Bunter,
who am I to make the rules?
If they be fools, why should I grumble?
It's bad enough the price
of Sudsless stock's about to tumble.

EXPLORING KROH

The first few days were wearing
as the Delegation struggled hard
to get its bearing.
The Crocs, who'd gone off to explore
two days before, had not returned.
All hoped they'd find some fish
or frogs to nurture them
while on the quest to test
their youthful and romantic notions,
and not resort to eating Krohtians.

The morning of Day Three,
Rip, Terry, and the Navajo,
along with Ken and Rex and Moe,
plus others of the Delegation,
spent several hours sightseeing,
appraising, gazing, making every kind
of critical evaluation of the planet's
present and potential worth
to all the money-lenders, speculators,
network television stations
and exporters of the Earth.

To get around,
they used a dozen souped-up LEMs
which ran on liquid nitrogen
and flew a few feet off the ground.

Their first stop was some distant towers,
structures built (as well as anyone could tell)
at least 3000 years before.
Alas, today they were as still as tombs,
with walls and rooms all falling down.
Murals on some parts still standing

were another revelation.
Kroh, they saw, once had a landscape
covered with thick vegetation.

Another wonder of the trip
was one small sandy strip
all strewn with scrap
where once the landing module of a ship,
in its so delicate pre-touchdown dance,
had failed its one and only chance
to miss a rock.

Said Ken, The modem that we use today
was knocked outside it by the shock.
It didn't break,
but suffered quite a brutal sanding.
The aliens inside the ship
were smashed to smithereens on landing.

While Ken was talking,
Terry, Rip and Rabbit Stalker
walked a little ways apart.
Then said the Navajo,
I'm tired of these tourist shows.
I want to talk with native Krohs.
But, Rab, said Rip,
you know the billion have no tongues.
If conversation
with the Krohtian nation's your intention,
you'll have to settle for the Menschen.

We Indians, said Stalker, have some other
methods of communication,
codes more secret even
than those used in World War II.
When I look down
and see the faces of a thousand
unborn Krohtians looking up

from underneath the ground,
although this soil is not my mother earth,
that sky up there is not my dad,
I know that I have more in common
with these Krohs who have no tongues,
than with so many men I've known
throughout my life, who had.

And then the Navajo knelt down
and started softly drumming with his hand
upon the Krohtian rocks and sand.
It was the ancient rhythm of the heart.
And while he drummed,
as if it heard and wanted to take part,
the Krohtian earth beneath his feet
resounded with the self-same beat.

Then Stalker took some sand
and let it sift between the fingers of his hand,
bent near, and listened
as each grain did whisper in his ear
the history...the now...the future of the Krohs,
three stages which were really one
so very long continuum.
And as he listened, tears fell from his eyes
for what was past, and present, and to come.

I think, said Terry, you have tapped into
the poetry and majesty of this strange land,
and maybe too, its tragedy.

THE FIRST POLLING

That afternoon, Economist Ben Carter
sat down with Ken and Rex and Moe.
Said he, Our Delegation was impressed
by what we saw today.
Your ancient cities show
what we would not have guessed:
that Krohtians once had what it takes
to work, and think, and plan and build.
We all were thrilled, for trade with Earth
should put you fellows on the track
to bring your former glories back.

But first, said Ben, I'd like to know
exactly what occurred up here
some thirty centuries ago.
Investors don't like mystery.
They don't care if your history
is black as tar, but hate surprises.
They'll want to know exactly what befell
your transportation system,
vegetation, and highrises.

Answered Ken, It has been rumored,
and our ancient scriptures tell,
of something that befell our planet
way back then. According to Apostle Mel,
it was a happening involving gods and men,
and afterwards
Kroh never was the same again.
(Though I should add,
another school of thought disputes this,
positing instead that one gigantic comet
made of ice and granite
put the kibosh on the planet.)

Now, whether Krohtians wish to go

the inter-global trading way
and see the place restored
to what it was before, I couldn't say.
But we could take a poll
and give the answer to you right away.

Then go for it, said Carter,
holding up his thumb.

So Ken and Moe did make some signs,
like twitch and sniff and sigh,
that instantly were taken up
by several Krohtians passing by,
and they sent on the signs
to other brethren far and wide
who understood this tongue.

Thus in an exponential way
the query went forth on its quest
toward east and north,
evoking yeas and nays across
the plains and upper half of Kroh,
then spread around the lower globe
to rise up from the south and west
and hop across to Ken and Moe.

We have the poll results,
announced the Mentians.
It's fifty percent pro and fifty contra
with a couple of abstentions.
Just who these hold-outs were
we do not know,
but one was certainly a duck,
one probably a Navajo.

Ben Carter was delighted. Fifty-fifty?
That was positively nifty.
They've cancelled themselves out,

thought he.
With no majority opinion to compel us,
we can do just what the hell
our own best interests tell us.

And then he said, I've got to go,
but is there anything you'd like to know?

Asked Moe, will beads and barter
still be part of any deal?

I wouldn't count on it, said Carter.
We're talking marketing for real.

BREAKFAST ON DAY FOUR

The morning of Day Four,
the Delegation chose once more
to breakfast out of doors.
The first to take their seats
upon some comfortably-placed stones,
were Sam and Dr. Fink,
Ned Bunter, Jack Perone
and Rabbit Stalker,
who had spent the night away,
but now had come
with two of his new Krohtian chums.

By this time everyone had heard
about the poll on inter-global trade
that showed a split decision.
And when the Duck,
with shiver, snort and cough
asked these two Krohtians
(who were eating eggs and manna

from a kind of little trough)
just how they'd voted, yes or no,
they burped right back
that one was contra, one was pro.

Said Dr. Fink, Okay,
perhaps the one who voted nay
can tell me what I've come
this long, long way to know.
Private Stalker,
kindly ask your Krohtian friend
who voted against economic progress
with its frenzies and rat races,
preferring, as he obviously must,
dry sand, hard rocks and stasis,
how he spends his day without the thrill
of watching on the TV screen
The World's Worst Motorcycle Chases,
without the bitter pill
of listening to lunatics all day
who say two hundred bucks an hour
is too much for them to pay,
of fighting medical malpractice lawsuits
brought by patients whom he's ired,
owing millions to a half a dozen lawyers
that he hired after finding
his insurance had expired
and whom he should have fired months ago.
In short, how does that Krohtian
pass the bloody day?

Now, this was something
that the Navajo already knew
and was prepared to say;
that life does not need
stress or aggravation,
or all-consuming passions
such as jealousy and hate,

or daily stats on robbery and killing,
to be fulfilling.
It was enough to celebrate
each moment of the day,
the miracle of how the sunlight
sits upon a rock,
the feel of sand between your toes
because you wear no sock or shoe,
the taste of manna wet with dew.

This Krohtian does not feel the need,
said Rabbit Stalker, for a god
who comes one day with miracles,
makes promises, then disappears,
so that no miracles are seen again
for several thousand years.
For Krohs, like Navajos,
see miracles around them on a daily basis.
Yet that ideal, which may sound Zen,
is what some men condemn as stasis.

At this the Shrink did sigh,
What's with this guy?
Did I come all the way to Kroh
to hear a Navajo explain how I should think?
Just which one is the shrink?
Does he believe he'll help me find
all sorts of things I buried long ago
deep down inside my heart and mind?

Then said the Duck,
This other Krohtian tells me,
since we landed on his planet, he
and half his people dream
of colored beads that shine like gems
and driving chopped-down, souped-up LEMs.
In short, there seems to be
a huge dichotomy of worldly notions

– much larger than I would have reckoned –
between the first half billion Krohtians
and the second.

That's not surprising, said Ned Bunter.
This morning, before breakfast,
I tested DNA from both these fellows,
finding in the one a Jewish gene
whose presence in a lot of others
I had previously noted.
In fact, I think that there's a link
between a Krohtian's chromosomes
and how he voted. For I'll admit
that all my findings seem to fit
that fifty-fifty polling split.

Now, whether half a billion Jewish genes
all cast their votes for inter-global dealing,
or whether they all favored stasis,
I've no intention of revealing,
fearing being called a racist.

Ned, you're right, said Dr. Fink.
Genetic influence on what a person thinks
is not a can of worms you ought to resurrect,
unless you want to hear the Duck
and every other TV pundit,
talk-show host and critic
label you politically incorrect,
or even worse, anti-Semitic.

I myself have always thought
we Jews enjoy a long tradition
of living life as fully as we're able,
enjoying music, travel
and material possessions
such as Cadillacs and sable.
Still, most of us believe it is our mission,

when we can, to lend a hand
at helping to preserve endangered species,
habitat, and public land.

Now, whether either tendency or trait
is in our DNA, I strongly doubt
but cannot know.
But if you think that Jewish genes
did influence the Krohtian vote,
then think again;
those genes did not come
just from *Jews* –
they came from *men*.

A CARTOGRAPHER IN LOVE

During breakfast,
while the griddle cakes were being buttered,
fresh eggs beaten,
and some strong opinions uttered,
Jack Perone had neither listened,
spoken, nor had eaten.
What kept him so apart?
It was his heart, his lovesick heart,
that fussed and fluttered
in unspeakable distress
and took his mind off all but Tess.

Oh, how in this strange world
was he to woo her?
The planet had no June,
no blue lagoon,
no small, discrete motel.
Why, hell, it didn't even have a moon.
But, maybe that was just as well,

for should she raise her lovely eyes
and see a moon she didn't recognize,
about one half the size of ours
or even smaller, it might appall her.

Last night he'd drawn a map of Kroh
and now removed it from his pocket.
Was this sufficient for a gift
or should he wait and buy a locket?
Then he recalled those lines of Swift
recounting how so long ago
geographers, in Afric maps,
with savage pictures filled their gaps,
and o'er unhabitable downs
placed elephants for want of towns.

His map was not at all like these,
for he had drawn it just to please.
Indeed, he'd filled Kroh's deserts, seas,
and other tracts he did not know
with flowers, hearts, and mistletoe.

Oh, Tessie, he so longed to say,
to be on Kroh and out of range
of earthly satellites
is like we lived some other day,
when GPS and GIS
were still two thousand years away,
when map-making was still an art,
cartographers in love with mystery
and the unknown,
not merely ignorant
of what could not as yet be shown.

If here on Kroh one really could live life
like way back then,
I'd use but chain or tape
(or simply stand some sixty-six

young foot-wide Krohtians nape to nape
to serve as my triangle bases).
Then I'd take you by the hand
and we would hie us overland
to distant places,
without compass or theodolite
since neither one was yet invented
(though, to shelter us at night
I think a small tent might be rented).
Tess, oh, Tess,
how happily we then would go,
seeing all the sides and angles
of our love and passion grow,
eating manna, drinking dew,
triangulating over Kroh.

THE NITTY GRITTY

Ben Carter and the General
sat down together at another table,
looking like a mini-junta.
Said Ben, I got the word from Rip,
who got it from the crew:
The food supply is running low
and in two days we'll have to go.

So, he continued,
we were sent here with a mission
and should come to some decision
as to whether Kroh is ripe for trade.
It's clear to me
this planet lacks a minimal economy,
but has the asset of a billion population,
all of them potential

workers and consumers.
This represents a demographic
similar to baby boomers.

So here's my plan.
We'll lend them...let me see,
ten billion dollars ought to be enough
to give the Krohs the wherewithal
to buy the stuff that Earth produces
(theme parks, pesticides, and such),
and charge them only ten percent
per annum interest. Clearly that's a deal
that any usurer would call a steal.
What collateral would we require?
None at all. We'll take their IOU
and shake their hand.
Should they default,
we'll simply confiscate their land.

Good shot, said Dora Battle, stroking
the bright ribbons on her chest.
Now, off the record, here's what *I* suggest.
If we discover Kroh has gold,
uranium, or other wealth,
we colonize the planet,
send the Army Corps of Engineers
to canalize and dam it,
and several thousand
Workfare employees to man it.
Then, to guarantee the whole thing clicks,
we'll add ten thousand G.I.'s to the mix.

Said Ben, Your scheme's first rate.
Pre-emption of another state
worked pretty well
for Belgians, Frogs and Brits,
who reaped enormous benefits
before they had to call it quits.

If we both colonize
and lend at ten percent, I'll bet
that in a thousand years,
if Krohs have freed themselves of debt,
they'll be as happy as today,
with no tears or regret.

I'm curious, said Dora Battle,
what Steve Clift, our resident Geologist,
has found beneath the Krohtian ground.
Our native peoples hate to mine uranium,
and tend to get most quarrelsome
when asked to lend their tribal lands
to store atomic waste.
But Krohs, I'm sure, would gladly do
the mining and the storing too
for beads made out of paste.

I like your style, said Carter.
There's not an angle you've neglected.
Any company that trades up here
will feel itself darn well protected.
Sending soldiers is a brilliant touch.
Not that the Krohtians could do much
to block the future we've projected.

Still, said Battle, to forestall
all unexpected glitches,
we'll have to win their hearts and minds
by promising them jobs and riches.
For if the Krohtians feel disquiet,
and any of them start to riot,
prime time television features
showing G.I.'s gunning down these
teddy-bearish creatures
might cause hitches.

I see your point, said Ben.

It's not as though the Krohs were black,
with bones stuck through their noses.
Should a gold mine boss or guard
shoot down a savage in New Guinea,
kill his wife and pickaninny,
who would know or give a hoot?
(Unless a bullet ricocheted
and hit some fellow in a suit.)
But as you say,
the Krohtians are too cute to shoot.

Exactly, said the General.
We mustn't be perceived
as causing *one* of them to die.
To keep them calm, we'll launch
an operation code-named 'Pacify'.
This means our propaganda
has to zero in on that objective
and be ten times more effective
than it was in Vietnam.
Disinformation should be handled by a guy
as quick to lie and smoothly verbal
as the Third Reich's Joseph Goebbels,
greedy and at home with schlock
as that ex-Aussi, Rupert Murdock,
able to manipulate
minds, hearts, ambitions and emotions
while speaking easily to Krohtians.
Impossible to find?
Well, we're in luck.
The one I have in mind
to pitch the riches to the Krohtians
is the Duck.
Now don't forget, she warned,
no word of this can be repeated.

Then Dora Battle looked around
and saw Cartographer Perone, seated

at a table all alone
like some abandoned sap.
Was this because the gal he loved
was taking a mid-morning nap
with that pragmatic guy
who wore that red and yellow tie?

We'll tap this fellow too, said she,
To draw some lines upon our map.

PLANTING CORN

Now that blast-off day was nigh,
McDonalduck was feeling torn
between the farm duck he was born
and the Duck he had become.

Late that morn,
the side of him that he did scorn
took out a can of unpopped corn,
and in a little plot of ground
planted kernels all around
(letting only three of four
slide down his bill into his craw).
All afternoon Sam oversaw his tiny plot
and fed it from his chamber pot.
By evening, fifty shoots were up
and over half he placed a cup.
Next morning, when the sun arose,
it was exactly as he'd feared;
the shoots he hadn't covered up
had disappeared.
And in their place?
That whitish, tell-tale trace.

It's clear, thought Sam,
if Krohs had pesticides instead of bugs,
and reasons to get off their tushes,
they could raise not only corn,
but beans, rose hips, and berry bushes.
To motivate them, I could buy their land
for colored beads,
lease it back to them to farm,
and, attentive to their needs,
sell them fertilizers,
pesticides and hybrid seeds.
Just paying back the interest on their debt
would exercise their backs and bones
and stop them sitting on these stones.

And yet...and yet...,
the Duck had to admit,
there was a certain charm in sitting on a rock
and watching how the morning sunlight lit
those little sprouts of green.
It took him back to duckling days
when he had not a dime,
but lots of time to dream
and watch the crops grow tall.
How well he could recall, with rue,
his brothers and his sisters too,
their joyful games, their happy quacks,
until the day they met the axe.

Why them instead of me? sighed Sam.
What was the matter?
Was it because I happened to be thinner
and they fatter?
And must I feel eternally a sinner
because I wasn't that poor schmuck
who got selected first for dinner?
He laughed, reflecting on his luck.

Just then, along came Dr. Fink.
Exclaimed the shrink,
Why, here's our famous anchor Duck,
helping Krohtian grasses grow.
You are, he said to Sam,
a most amazing dude,
so please don't think me rude
if I should say
I'd love to get inside your mind
and see what guilts and traumas
a Psychiatrist might find
in someone raised for food.
Could that account for
your obsessive appetite for wealth?

Sighed Sam, just managing
to hide his grin,
Oh, Doctor Fink, you can't imagine
what a state I'm in.
It's starting to affect my health.
The more I earn,
the more I yearn to earn some more.
Money is a terrible addiction,
yet no one seems to care
about this millionaires' affliction.
The government has even ruled
that if I take a wife,
every egg of our production
is an IRS deduction.

I have no need for all this money.
Ducks don't wear Italian shoes
and rarely touch hard drugs or booze.
The only time my money's not a bore
is when I speculate on stock and get a lock
on gaining several million more.

Said Harry Fink, I feel your pain.

The great Voltaire was right as rain
when he observed
two centuries and more ago,
the way for man or duck to live
is how you've done it here on Kroh:
spreading good organic dung
to make your garden grow.
I'll bet it's crossed your mind
to stay right here
and say goodbye to CBA
and all the fame and fortune
that you once held dear.

At this, Sam racked his brain
for some sarcastic comment
he could offer as reply.
But every time he found what seemed
a perfect one to try,
some other duck within him
whispered that it was a lie.

RETURN OF THE CROCS

That afternoon there was a stir
when Lash and Coca,
both with shining eyes and glowing leather,
reappeared together.
They weren't alone.
Gently held in Coca's jaws
were twenty little crocodiles,
all newly hatched and cute as blazes.

This planet constantly amazes,
said the happy mom.
We never saw so many fish and frogs
as in the Krohtian rivers and the oceans.

All day the waters swarm with tasty bugs
that go ashore at night
in one big mass migration
to gobble up the vegetation.
By dawn they're back,
all fat and doubly nutritious,
numerous as krill,
full of chlorophyll,
and just delicious.

Said Lash, we want to tell you
we've decided to remain on Kroh.
Habitat is everything to crocs,
and Krohtian waters are a vast lunch box
for us and all our sons and daughters.
So now we have to catch the tide,
but thanks to all of you
and to the Menschen and the Krohs,
and to the U.S taxpayers
who underwrote our ride.
Please send our love and greetings
to our families and friends in YO,
but now we have to go.

And as the Delegation waved goodbyes
and wiped their eyes,
the Crocs climbed down
into the old, abandoned
transportation system underground
and swam away.

And never were they seen again
by men.

THE WARNING

I think, said Mentian Ken to blacker Mike,
as they and Moe
strolled through the ancient towers,
that in the past 3000 years
there was less change on Kroh
than since you fellows came five days ago.
Now every Mentian has a name,
and there's a 50-50 split
among the billion, hitherto so closely knit.

And now what do we learn?
That we have genes that give us rights
the Rabbi calls 'return'.
She says this means that Moe, and I,
plus some five hundred million,
can go to Earth
and live upon a piece of land
whose rocks and sand
are more or less exactly
what we have already here to hand.

I think I'd like to go, said Moe,
but maybe I should ask our buddy, Mike,
for his more worldly-wise insight.

Smiled Michael Jones,
I should point out that 'Mike', like 'Ike',
rhymes less well with 'insight',
than 'Dwight'.

That said, said he, I might suggest
that here on Kroh
you Menschen have it made.
You are a definite minority
but seem to wield authority,
while down on Earth you all would be

routinely pestered,
even interned or sequestered
by the Immigration Service,
circumstantially suspected
by the troopers and the cops,
but worst of all, subjected to
a Barbara Walters interview.
After which they'd pull out all the stops
and kick you off the planet
and/or stick you in a zoo.
It's not because each one of you
has genes that say you are a Jew.
That wouldn't fly today
(although I've heard some buzz
along those lines about the FBI and CIA),
but mainly it's because you're you, not they.

Said Ken, I think we ought to stay right here.
We got some shivers, shrugs and quacks
a little while ago
that spread in seconds over Kroh
and promised us good jobs and riches
if we Krohtians don't cause glitches
in the setting up of inter-global trade.
They want us to accept huge loans,
brigades of army engineers,
and then, to get us off the stones
and exercise our backs and bones,
they'll buy our land with colored beads
and rent it back so we can work it,
tax us only eighty-five percent
so we won't shirk it,
then sell us hog-farm sludge well laced
with very fresh atomic waste,
non-reproductive hybrid seeds,
and pesticides to kill our bugs.
And that was just the quacks and shrugs.

Asked Mike, What kind of glitches
do they fear?

Said Ken, That wasn't clear.
They seem to want to keep us quiet,
win our hearts so we don't riot
or turn upon them like some Brutus.
And if we don't do any of that stuff,
they promise not to shoot us.

Said Moe, I think that's fair enough.

But promises, warned Mike,
can easily be broken,
solemn pledges be misspoken;
I should know.
And furthermore, dear Ken and Moe,
I have to tell you, as a U.S. Politician
and a sometime token black,
you shouldn't trust
one shiver, shrug or quack
these Earthlings may have
signed or spoken,
unless you definitely know
the signals that you get have come
directly from
that Navajo.

THE 50-GALLON DRUM

I like your product,
Tessie Rubble told the CEO.
Our test went off without a hitch.
Last night Bill James and I…
Bill's that pragmatic, theme-park guy.

You may have seen us in a LEM....

Said Arnie Robb, Oh, was that Bill?
I thought it was that Jack Perone.

Oh, no, laughed Tess.
If you had seen the map Jack drew for me,
you'd know he's just a clown.
The map showed half the globe of Kroh
with elephants in place of towns
and Krohtians dressed in funny gowns
with bones stuck through their noses.
(And trust me, Arn, those teddy bears
weren't out to smell the roses.)
But weirder than the Krohs' attire
was the way he drew this planet
bound around with thick barbed wire.
I have a hunch Jack did aspire once
to be my heart's desire, but....
Then Tessie tapped her head.
I guess he lost it.
We found the map upon my bed
where he had tossed it.

That figures, said the CEO.
I saw Jack just a while ago
working with the General and Carter.
He had a look upon his face
like some poor martyr.

I wouldn't be surprised, said Tess.
In any case, last night
Bill James and I dripped just a drop
of your fine pesticide upon the ground,
then left and came back in an hour.
For thousands of square feet around
no living insect could be found.
This morning, when the sun arose,

well, praise the Lord,
it was a different scene.
The bug-free land was turning green
and gone was that odd, whitish trace.

I'll tell you what, continued Tess,
if pesticides can rid this place
of everything that crawls,
as soon as I get back to Earth
I'll get out floor plans that I made
for highrise condos, burbs, and malls,
and from those plans I'll pre-sell
living and commercial space.
Then in a year I'll come back here
and thoroughly revamp this place.

Said Robb, it really breaks all norms
how well my pesticide performs.
I sometimes like to sit and watch
the miracle of how it kills.
Some say rapacious insects are a plague
that comes from God on high
to punish kings with stubborn wills.
I don't know why they came to Kroh,
but what the hell, that's in the past.

Today, I heard the latest poll shows
Krohs have made a stand at last
and will be buying all they need,
from Bill's theme parks to hybrid seed.
I guess we gave them one great loan.
This means, of course,
the Krohs will live forever and a day
in landless squalor,
working to repay each dollar.
And that is how it *should* be, for,
'If there be rich there must be poor'.

That said, I hope they celebrate
their new-found Krohtian solvency
with one big all-out spending spree.
Then I won't have to take
these fifty gallons home with me,
for as you see,
this old drum may start leaking.

Don't worry about that, said Tess.
If they don't want it,
you can sell your pesticide to me.
It's exactly what I'm seeking.

THE NAVAJO'S DILEMMA

Day Seven had been chosen
for the blast-off back to Earth.
The day before they were to go,
Terry, Rip and Rabbit Stalker
took a walk together
that would be their last on Kroh.
Suddenly the Navajo,
looking terribly distressed,
stopped and turned.
I've got to quit the army, he confessed.
It stands for everything I'm not.

Well, hey, said Rip,
if you want out, I know a way.
Just tell the General you're gay.

Laughed Rab, I never thought of that.
And then the laughter left his face.
But I can't lie, he said. In any case,
I think she'll find a better reason,

something that the State calls treason.

Rip and Terry plainly saw
this wasn't meant to be a joke.
Was Rabbit under some delusion?
What had happened to provoke
his frightening conclusion?

Yesterday, he told his friends,
I happened to receive a message –
quacks and shrugs and other motions
sent by Sam to all the Krohtians –
telling about jobs and riches,
loans and armies, hogs and glitches.
But then it told them something stranger:
To avoid their being shot,
they mustn't riot or cause hitches.
Judging from the feedback that I got,
the Krohtians understood the good,
but not the danger.

That litany of greed I intercepted
wasn't master-minded by the Duck.
Most of it was cooked up
by the General and Carter.
And now the latest polling figures show
their gambit did succeed;
it killed the 50-50 split,
for every Krohtian bit, and voted pro.
If that vote is allowed to stand,
Earthlings will usurp this land.

Then Rab went on,
I had a word with blacker Mike,
and we agreed that only those
who know how to communicate with Krohs
can turn the vote around,
and that means me.

And so today I plan to drum my message
to the ground and sky,
holler, dance, and slap my thigh
and tell the Krohs that if they follow
where the white man leads,
they'll lose their land and die.

Then Stalker chuckled bitterly,
I'm sure that when the General
sees I've undone the strategy
that she's begun, she'll call it treason.

But Rab, said Ter,
she can't declare an open season
on all Indians who dance,
or ask a jury to convict a Navajo
for drumming.
You'll leave no paper trail, and so
what judge or jury possibly could know
what messages your thumping sent,
much less what that Duck's shrugs
had meant?

I hope you're right, replied the Navajo.
I'd hate to spend my life inside a cell.
But what the hell?
There's nothing better that I have to do today
than dance and shout and holler,
and tell a billion Krohs
about the evil Yankee dollar,
and warn this native people
that the white men have the guns, and shoot,
have the poisons, and pollute,
and Krohtians shouldn't give two hoots
for all the promises they give.

For if those teddy-bearish creatures

want to keep their land and live,
they can't keep quiet.
They have to tell their story
on the prime time news,
stand in front of TV crews,
and riot, riot, riot.

THE FIGHT FOR HEARTS AND MINDS

The final afternoon on Kroh
was one more lovely day like every other,
making people want to bow
to strangers in the street, and say,
Oh, sister, brother,
have you ever breathed an air so sweet?
Only there was not one stranger,
and no street, nor anyone to greet,
except some Delegation members
and some Krohtians
and some Mentians.

The Navajo walked off alone
across a mile of sand and stone
until he found a spot
where unborn Krohtian faces
peered from underneath the ground.
And there he found a place to stand
between the sand and sky
(that wasn't on some fetal eye),
a place where he could drum and dance
and plead the cause, and warn all Kroh
to cancel out the vote of pro.

And dance he did, and drum and holler
as he never had before.

And every Krohtian passing by
took up each beat and motion,
passing on the precious mantra
over sand and rock and ocean.
And when the vote came back
it was one hundred percent contra.

The first to learn the worst
among the Earthlings was McDonaldduck.
And though he tried to cause a rally,
and, with shiver, shrug and quack,
turn the tide and get the former tally back,
he had no luck. Alas, this time the Duck,
despite his skill, was unable to will,
or in some way persuade,
a single Kroh or Mentian
to cast his vote again for trade
or even military intervention.

Sighed he, who had to tell
the General and Carter
that their inter-global baby
was a definite non-starter,
I hope the time is past
when bearers of bad news
were killed or beaten,
or, when the messengers were ducks,
routinely eaten.

DAY SEVEN –- ESCAPE FROM KROH

Next morning on arising,
the Delegation sensed a vague disquiet
over Kroh. By nine
there were some signs of riot.

Krohtians, using unambiguous
and graphic motions,
told the Earthlings
they should leave without delay.

Eating breakfast in the dining bay,
Delegation members looked out through
the panoramic windows
at the milling Krohtian scene.
Finishing her Ovaltine,
the General observed, It's bad;
the Krohs are even cuter when they're mad.
And then she threw an angry look
at Sam McDonalduck,
while thinking, Since we've lost
the Krohtian hearts and minds
by trusting that insipid bird,
a bird we should have cooked
with all his quacks and shrugs,
we'll have to try a different tack
to win Kroh back,
like tourism and drugs.
And as for Private Stalker,
I see no reason
not to try the kid for treason.

Just then, the young Astronomer,
announcing that the countdown had begun,
saw two figures heading toward
the space ship at a run.
Oh, damn! cried Rip.
I didn't realize anyone was missing.

Said Sam, that looks like you-know-who.
As like as not,
the two went off to do some kissing.
Then suddenly remembering
what he'd forgot,

Sam ran to beat the doctor to the pot.

And while the tardy humans
hurried through the ever-thicker crowd
of irate Krohtians, climbed into the ship,
and quickly zipped their Velcro on,
still others joined Mcdonalduck
on line to use the john.
The crew, who had already been and gone,
went through their pre-flight checklist,
finding all the systems GO.

Then Rip stood up again
and with a solemn face, he said,
We came to Kroh
in what I thought was peace.
But we brought war instead.
We brought division
to a happily united race.
And what is more,
in this strange cultural collision
we acted like a brute.
And so it's fitting that we leave here
empty-handed and in disrepute,
thanking all our lucky stars
the Krohtians have no guns to shoot.

Now, since this is my ship,
and I am in command, please understand
I will not tolerate
the slightest angry look or reprimand,
or any talk of sabotage or treason,
by any one for any reason.
Back on Earth I'll write up my report,
but now I'll ask McDonalduck,
as soon as we get underway,
to note down everyone's opinion
on the outcome of our mission.

I'd like your honest take,
so please feel free to make
the strongest case for your position.
Oh, and by the way,
our Poet's twenty-one today,
so later we'll have cake.

Then Rip sent off a reassuring grin
toward Ter and Rab and blacker Mike.
And as the four friends waited
for the final countdown to begin,
they looked out at the Krohtian world
of sand and stone,
and at those gentle,
now so-troubled people
they'd so briefly known.
And all four tried, in vain, to spot
among those soft, protesting millions
their dear friends, Ken, Rex, and Moe,
whose names would evermore be lost
in that vast silence that was Kroh.

Then as the space ship fired up
and slowly started its ascension,
they closed their eyes
and said goodbyes
to all the billion,
and the Menschen.

PART THREE:

THE RETURN

THE INTERVIEWS

McDonalduck was stressed.
Thought he, It's such a bummer.
How could a pro like me
be second-bested by a drummer?

But when the pressure
of the take-off blast had passed,
and Sam recalled the interviewing task
Rip had suggested,
he got his bearings back
and felt revitalized and rested.

The first he wished to interview
was Steven Clift
of Continental Plate & Drift.
McDonalduck was sure
that if the man had located
some diamonds or some ore,
his company would find a way
to get back up to Kroh and drill
(no matter whom they had to kill),
and then their stock would head uphill.

But, alas, though Sam
used all his duckish charm
and journalistic skill
to feign disinterest,
angle in, and ask his question,
all he got was Steve Clift's
rude suggestion
as to where the Duck could stick his bill.

Thought Sam, Oh, well,
when insiders won't play along,
by now I know the drill.
I'll sell off every share,

and next time that I'm on the air
I'll drop a hint that Continental Plate
found not one glint of ore on Kroh.
And when their stock can't take the blow,
and crashes, what the heck;
I'll buy five thousand shares on spec.

*　　*　　*

Examining the other faces in the room,
the Duck could see that it would be
a waste of time approaching
either Battle or Ben Carter
whose expressions were a glower.
Sam already knew what those two
thought about the mission,
and that they might prefer to talk about
or, better yet, devour,
tasty *canard a l'orange*
or duck in sweet and sour.

Mike Jones, the White,
was also looking dour.
He'd nearly finished up the trip,
was on the brink of fame,
could almost see the ticker tape
and hear the crowd shout out his name.
So why, asked Sam, looked he so grim?

Because, Mike growled,
there was that shadow stalking him;
a blacker Mike so well connected,
he could instantly reverse a poll
and get himself elected.

But Sam, I've learned a lot from you.
If I can raise sufficient bucks,
buy time on television,

manipulate the voters' minds
and cause division with my lies,
I'll have a chance with either slogan:
I Like Whites or He Wikes Guys.

Said Sam, Mike Jones, I like your pluck.
Your polarizing views
will grab the media's attention.
But play it cool. Don't push your luck
by seeking votes from large minorities
or Menschen.

*   *   *

Sam glanced around
for someone else to interview,
and noticed Jack Perone
sitting all alone, sketching on a pad.
He looked so sad,
McDonalduck was keen to know
exactly what was on his mind.

Why, nothing special, answered Jack.
I've been assigned
to draw a map of Kroh.

But when he showed the map to Sam,
the Duck was taken utterly aback.
Said he, You've drawn these spheres
completely black.

Not so, said Jack.
If you enlarge these circles
to the size of Kroh,
you'll see a grid which demarcates
a billion fenced-off lots.
Each square is then a tiny plot
on which one teddy bear could squat.

This represents a real breakthrough for me,
who stupidly had hoped one day
to wield a huge eraser,
and rub away the lines
and other demarcations
separating plots of land
that men call 'mine' or 'nations'.
But when I learned
I'd nevermore embrace her....
And he dissolved in tears.

Sam took another look
at Jack's strange hemispheres.
Thought he, The fellow's lost it.
He must imagine half the Krohtians
would agree to live on oceans,
for that's how he's crisscrossed it.
Then asked the Duck,
Just who assigned this task to you?

Why *I* did, sobbing Jack replied.
Cartographers don't work on spec.
We have our pride.

Heh, heh, said Sam. I guess I'll go
and interview the CEO.
Then, wishing Perone lots of luck,
away Sam snuck on tippy toe,
as quietly as one could go
on webbed feet shod with thick Velcro.

*   *   *

But finding Robb deep in a huddle
with Bill James and Tessie Rubble,
Sam walked across to talk to Bunter.
Hey, Ned, he said, how goes it with
our microbe hunter?

You wouldn't want to know, said Ned.
If Krohs wore clothes
I would have made a killing.
And yet, I must admit,
my efforts in genetics
weren't completely unfulfilling.
The DNA did positively show
that roughly three millennia ago
some Hebrews fooled around on Kroh.
Sam, you recall the Rabbi's notion
she'd repatriate each Krohtian
having Jewish genes?
Well, then she ran into a glitch
that sabotaged her noble vision.
She looked at several thousand Krohs
and saw no place for circumcision.

Shrugged he, What could I say?
It's something of a mystery.
For just between you, Sam, and me,
I've never seen one in the john
and have no inkling how they pee,
much less how Krohtians get it on.
I only know if she'd stood firm
in her intention,
she might have moved to Tel Aviv
five hundred million plus the Menschen.

Did any of them want to go?

I think one did. His name was Moe.
It's possible he changed his mind.
In any case, they all got left behind.
But now I find those ancient Jews
did not only infuse
the Krohtian locals with their seed,
they may have left behind some clues

on how they managed to achieve
their inter-global cruise. Indeed,
Tom Beal says ancient books reveal
what happened on the planet
thirty centuries ago.

Hey, that's a major scoop, cried Sam.
I'll interview Tom Beal right now.

No, no, said Ned.
Hold off a bit on him and Schwister.
I just passed by the reading nook
when Beal, our crook,
lay down his book,
gave Becky an unfathomable look,
then took her in his arms...
and kissed her.

*   *   *

When Dr. Fink saw Sam approach,
he smiled most cordially.
McDonalduck, forgive me
that I beat you to the pot.
That said, I bet you felt some dread
abandoning your grassy plot.

Said Sam, My cornfield's history.
Last night marauding insects
ate the roots and shoots
and left their trace
on sand and rock. Then he went on,
So, doc, aside from visiting the john,
how did it go?

Said Fink, well, Sam,
my theory that the Krohtian ego
crashed some thirty centuries ago

is still in doubt, although I think
the revelations of Tom Beal,
which he says he will soon unseal,
may lay that matter finally to rest.

As for my other quest,
before the Crocs swam on their way,
Lash told me that my favorite show,
The World's Worst Alligator Races,
is but fakery and stunts.
Hearing this, I felt like such a dunce
I swore I'd never watch the tube again.
But what the hell.
I learned on Kroh that some men
get along quite well
without that TV high.
And one day, using yoga, Zen,
or medication, so might I.

Now, would a space trip also help
my nutty clientele?
Perhaps to some degree.
But I'd prefer to see on Kroh
those litigation lawyers
that my clientele unleashed on me.
I'd have them live on manna
that they'd chip from off the rocks,
and when they're late to Krohtian courts,
have Krohtian enzymes clean their clocks.

McDonalduck, had I been born a waterfowl,
a wild and willful goose,
I'd fly about and loose my poop
on every lawyer's lawn and roof.
And when they sued me,
needing proof to back their words,
they'd have to plead before the judge
with briefcases stuffed full of turds.

Said Sam, Some say that shrinks are nuts,
but I have never heard
a human speak so cogently
the wisdom of the birds.

*   *   *

Stalker, Wright, and blacker Mike
were sitting all together
when McDonalduck came over.
Said Sam, a little sheepishly,
I guess you know the drill.

To which Mike Jones replied,
Hey man, we bear you no ill will.
You've got your job to do
and we've got lots to say,
so open up your bill
and interview away.

The Duck then turned to Terry Wright.
Said Sam, You've now spent
twenty-one years to the day
outside that smokey womb,
and since you aren't interred in any tomb
and obviously haven't died,
can we assume
you found a better world on Kroh?

A *better* one? the Poet sighed.
And then he answered with a smile,
A Mentian gave me some advice.
He had no name, and no profession either.
He said to me, If there be rich
there must be poor,
and poor is something we abhor,
so we have neither.

I think, continued Ter,
when we draw boundaries, compare,
and carry through the universe
judgmental and divisive words
like better and like worse, or rich and poor,
or when we speak
of good and bad or straight and gay,
eventually we lose our way
and know not what we seek.

And what is that, asked Sam?

Why love, of course, said Terry Wright.
When we find love, as I have done,
to paraphrase Walt Whitman's line,
the prize we *really* sought, is won.

As Terry spoke, Sam felt a lump
choke up his throat
and something wet invade his eye.
To stall for time,
he blindly jotted down a note.
But when he blinked away his tears
and looked at what it said,
he was amazed to find the jotting read:
*A duck that's raised for food
must never fall in love.*

And suddenly Sam absolutely knew
the only ducks that can and do
are those that fly high up above,
are wild and free,
And not, Sam told himself,
domesticated fowl like me.
My brothers, sisters, dad, and mom
were axed and plucked before my eyes.
Why heck, I hardly knew my mother's peck.

Can fear of losing one I've wooed
be why I never loved a duck
or raised a brood,
and am instead obsessed
by fame and fortune, power, and fine food?
There has to be a link.
Tonight I'll mention my epiphany to Dr. Fink.
He'll know what to conclude.

Then suddenly Sam struck his brow
in disbelief and dumb despair.
Had he been blind or lost his mind?
The truth had always been right there
in that so ancient barnyard rule:
Duck, love no duck,
unless thou wouldst be Fortune's fool.

When Sam had wiped away his tears
and felt more self-composed,
he turned to blacker Mike and said,
The whiter competition fears
that with your Navajo connection
you'll ace the polls and win election.

Hey, man, laughed Mike,
his campaign's cool.
So far he's followed every rule.
He's done part one, the trip to space,
so voters know his name and face.
And now, if he'd just vegetate
awaiting that November date –
not give you fellows of the fourth estate
the chance to crucify his ass
for, say, confusing Malta
with the Khyber Pass
or hound him for some carnal sin –
who knows, the sucker might just win.

That said, do I believe my buddy, Rab,
will help me in my quest
to be a two-year guest
at that Rotunda on the Hill?
Why yes. I think he will.

At this, up spoke the Navajo.
Said he, The question is, could I
create the same effect on Earth
as earlier I did on Kroh?
I'm not so sure, for even though
the promises of jobs and riches
flowing from the whiter Jones
would sound familiar,
like those pitches to the Krohs.

And even with you, Sam,
each evening on the TV screen,
quacking lines you read off
electronic monitors behind the scene
(lines written, by the way,
by corporations backing
that political machine
that backs the General and Carter,
corporations chaired by men
so greedy to increase their power
and their bottom lines
that even Billy James would blush
and fall into confusion
seeing pragmatism carried to
its logical conclusion).

And even though our blacker Mike
would take the side
of cleaner air and earth and water,
good education and equality
for every race and creed,
and I, supporting him, would beat my drum

to save our Earth for those there now
and those to come, as I have done
to save the Krohtian world from human greed,
the only difference that I see
in what will happen down on Earth
from what has happened up on Kroh,
is that not five percent will heed
the drumbeats of a Navajo.

Responded Sam,
I don't know where the two of you
picked up your cynical
and jaundiced views.
They surely didn't come
from watching TV nightly news.
Mine is a proud profession,
and our viewers are not dupes.
When CBA occasionally stoops
to pander to the blood thirst of the mob,
admittedly, a journalist must play along
or lose his job, and thus his pay,
which in my case
is thirty thousand bucks a day.
But may I say, an anchor Duck like me
still tries to balance fantasies
arising from his arrant greed
with ordinary social need,
and, despite what you two guys insinuate,
will listen quite objectively
to any Jones v. Jones debate.

*   *   *

Bill James and Tess,
who had been talking hard and fast
about a subject
that was anybody's guess,
as Sam approached were talking less.

Said he, Hey, Tess and Bill,
for just a moment there
I thought you'd given us the slip
and were about to miss the ship.
Did the riot of the Krohtians
alter any of your notions
about real estate development on Kroh?

Not very likely, Tess replied.
Sam, once you get to know them,
Krohs are sweethearts deep inside,
and full of hugs.
The only problem was the bugs.
But then I bought some pesticide
from Arnie Robb, which, with God's help,
should do the job.

Said Sam, But how do you propose
to get permission from the Krohs
to spread the poison on their land?

Laughed Tess, You mean that awful sand?
Oh, we were sure they wouldn't mind,
and since we didn't want to leave behind
that leaky drum,
Bill James and I sent all that goo
direct to where the bugs by day abound.
We poured it down that old, abandoned
transportation system underground
and threw the drum in too.
It ought real quick to rid the place
of all the things that creep and crawl
and leave a whitish trace on rocks,
and also finish off those Crocs.

I see, said Sam, who felt another tear
well up into his eye.
How come today his tears

were coming one by one un-dry?
And since some tears
had launched him in his fabulous career,
did these tears mean the end was near?

Sam turned his head
to see if anyone had overheard
what Tess had said,
but not another in the room
seemed suddenly beset by gloom.
Was this a scoop?
And if it was, how come
he wished to keep it mum
from all the others in the group?

So, guys, you did that
just before we blasted off?

That's right, said Bill.
We figure in a year or so,
when Tess and I return to Kroh
to do the building that we've planned,
there shouldn't be a bug alive
the length and breadth of Krohtianland.

Just then a member of the crew
arrived to say that lunch was on the way
and that the special of the day
was lobster stew.

So Tess stood up and took Bill's arm
as lovingly as bride takes groom,
and all the others rose as one
and headed for the dining room.

APERITIF TIME

Toward five o'clock, and following a snooze,
McDonalduck checked off his interviews
and found that there remained
no huge selection.
Tom Beal and Becky Schwister
had both looked different over lunch,
radiant and rested.
He found them in the reading nook,
not deep in books about the holy lands
or Virgin Mary, but holding hands
and sipping sherry.

You guys seem laid back,
said the Duck. Did you discover
something on the planet Kroh
the rest of us might like to know?

At this, the two exchanged a smile.
We'll tell you in a while, said Beal.
Tonight the two of us plan to reveal
our textual discoveries, and maybe more.

Then Becky said, Because we choose
to share our revelations
with the total Delegation,
we won't be giving interviews,
but plan to take the floor.
So I'm afraid you'll lose your scoop.

That's cool with me, Sam told her.
Perhaps I'm getting older,
but being first to get a story
doesn't seem the path to glory
that it did before.
I think that there's a duck
deep down inside of me

who more and more
is gaining the ascendancy,
and telling me there's better things in life
than getting a good scoop,
and one of them is having a good poop.

Perhaps when this strange trip is done
and I return to Washington,
I'll quit my job at CBA and buy a little farm.
And on that farm I'll be the master,
and will let no harm and no disaster
come to any duck in my purview,
or any sheep or hen or cow.
And then I'll hire somebody to steer the plow
and I will plant some corn.
And then I'll find a barnyard duck to love,
and when our duckling brood is born
I'll give them hugs and pecks
and write them yearly birthday checks
for maybe ten or twenty bucks.
Then next to their old dad,
in every way that can be had,
they'll be the wealthiest of ducks.

PRELUDE TO A GOSPEL

That evening, the entire Delegation
met together in the living bay
to find out what the Reverend and Rabbi
had to say. The mood was generally gay.
Most Delegation members,
happy to be on their way,
were glad they'd come.
Even Dora Battle and Ben Carter,
who all the morning looked so glum,

had thoroughly enjoyed the lobster stew,
had quaffed each one three pints of brew
and eaten cake and ice cream too.

At the stroke of nine,
Tom Beal and Becky Schwister
took the floor. Said he,
I know some rumors have been spread
concerning Beck and me.
I'd like to put them now to bed.
When we get home, we're getting wed.

He paused, to let the loud applause
die down, and then he said,
About ten days ago, my future bride and I
stood here together, side by side,
ready to deride the other's sacred vision
across that great divide
men call religion.

But during our sojourn on Kroh
we got to know a Mentian
who became our guru and our mentor.
It wasn't Ken or Moe or Rex,
he had no name, no sex,
but all the same, he did exist.
And when I found a revelation
in an ancient text
that seemed to negate all I'd ever learned
about my God, my Faith, and my Salvation,
I went to him and asked what I should do.

And he advised that for one day
I use no words like Christian and like Jew,
like Beal and Schwister, love and hate,
or brother/sister, father/son,
to see if I could then relate
to what he had to say,

which was, that Everything is One.

So I enlisted Becky's help,
and after talking for a day,
taking care to keep those harmful nouns
and adjectives at bay,
and concentrating on
the words that people say
to bring them close to one another,
we found a harmony
like we had never known before
with any other.

And when I held Beck in my arms
and looked down at her many charms,
then over at that ancient text,
the story that it told
no longer seemed a threat,
but only served to show
that life is much more interesting
than one could ever know.

And so, I think no matter what
we truly do believe,
we have to sometimes put it all aside
so we can change and grow.
For in the universe of heart and soul,
with all its secret, undiscovered places,
there is no room
for boundaries or stasis.

And now, if you'll all settle down
and listen open-mindedly and well,
the Rabbi will read from a gospel
written thirty centuries ago
by someone called Apostle Mel.

THE GOSPEL ACCORDING TO MEL

Dear Future Reader: Known to my contemporaries as Mel the Mummer, I set down these lines bearing witness to certain startling events that occurred recently in Jerusalem and on this planet. I do this so you will know the full truth concerning a group of young men who traveled here with their leader, Jesus of Jerusalem.

The Birth of Jesus

There lived in Jerusalem at that time a young woman named Linda, daughter of Philip and Susan. Linda was a comely maid and deeply devoted to the Lord. Her devotions attracted God's attention. One night God came to her in a dream and told her to fear not, for she would give birth to a son whom she would name Jesus. Jesus would grow up to be King of Israel and Judah, and King of the Jews.

And so it came to pass that Linda gave birth to a son. But because she had no husband, when her parents died she was obliged to live in the fields and forests among shepherds and wood choppers. Young Jesus, shunning such mindless labors and not wishing to become a rabbi either, joined a group of performing acrobats, musicians, magicians and mummers. They gave performances throughout the land in exchange for coins, food, or a place near the fire.

When God saw the sissified work Jesus was doing, he decided to throw all his heavenly weight behind young David. With the help of the Lord, David killed many thousands because God made him victorious everywhere.

When Jesus saw that the Lord God Almighty preferred that murderous, womanizing toady to his own son, he was saddened.

The Miracles of Jesus

Jesus was the best magician ever seen in Palestine. He could place a man in a box made of hard cedar, then cut the box through the middle without causing a drop of blood to flow. All who saw this knew God was working in Jesus, and not the Devil, or the man in the box would surely have died. So they did not persecute Jesus as a disciple of Satan.

An even more impressive trick Jesus practiced was levitation. On most days of the year, Jesus could levitate himself above the treetops. On Passover, he could levitate even higher than that.

The Parable of the Prodigal Son

Jesus traveled with his group and became famous throughout the land for his magic and parables. One story told of a father who joyfully welcomed back his wasteful, extravagant son who had been gone for years. He even killed the fatted calf to feast his son's return. When his hard-working, obedient, elder son complained, the father replied, "You have always been here with me, but he was lost and now is found, so he is even more precious."

After telling this story, Jesus would ask a wealthy man in the crowd to count out ten coins and make a fist around them. Then Jesus would pass his hands over the man's fist. When the man opened his hand, he would find only nine coins. The man would become furious and start to berate Jesus. Then Jesus would reach up and remove the missing coin from the man's nose and give it back to him.

The man would be so joyful at the return of his coin, he would give Jesus two or three coins out of pure gratitude.

Jesus Cures a Hideous Skin Disease

As famous as Jesus became in the land, God would still not acknowledge his son. The Lord remained at the side of David, helping him kill tens of thousands. Jesus felt God was only being that nice to David to make a point.

One day a man with a disgusting skin disease threw himself at the feet of Jesus and begged him to cure him. By good luck, Jesus suffered from the same skin ailment and carried at all times a small jar containing a balm his mother prepared from herbs. Jesus rubbed some on the man's sores and the itching stopped immediately. Two days later the rash was gone.

The man told everyone about the miraculous cure. He found Jesus' mother, Linda, and purchased a jar of balm from her.

After that, Linda stopped washing shepherds' cloaks and began selling her 'miracle cure' to the thousands suffering from hideous skin diseases. After seven years she was able to retire to a cottage on the Sea of Galilee where she lived comfortably the rest of her life.

The Silence of God

Meanwhile, God remained silent. Jesus felt he had to do something really big to impress his father with his brains and devotion. One day Jesus gathered his friends around him and made them his Disciples. He told them he was going to levitate to the Seat of God, and asked them to come along. As Jesus was the only 'star' of their touring company, and without him they might starve, all twelve agreed.

En Route to the Seat of God

At noon on the day of the Vernal Equinox, Jesus and his twelve disciples lay down side by side in a large field, held hands, and closed their eyes. Levitation was Jesus' best magic trick. He never disclosed how he did any of his tricks, least of all this one.

Suddenly the group could feel no ground beneath them. Thrilled, they kept their eyes tightly shut. Light turned to darkness, warmth into a deep cold like they had never known. It put them into a profound sleep and they did not know how much time passed before they awakened again.

When they opened their eyes, they were in a different place. Tall, slender towers stood in the near distance. Inhabiting this new land was a small, plump race with yellowish hair all over them. They did not look very kosher.

The inhabitants did not speak, but took the strangers to their city by means of an underground transportation system, and gave them food, drink, and water for bathing.

Among the Disciples was one who would have been a famous mathematician if he had not given up his studies to become a juggler. He calculated that they were on a celestial body halfway between Jerusalem and the Seat of God. So they named the planet Midway and settled down for a while.

Midway

Jesus and his Disciples were given comfortable rooms on the fifth floor of one of the towers. The first evening two Angels came to their door. The Angels told Jesus to return whence he had come, because, actually, the Seat of God was just an expression, a mathematical expression, not a chair, and if they did ever find it they would have no place to sit, or even stand.

But Jesus told them he would stay on Midway one week, or two, and then decide what to do. So the Angels went away. In the days to follow, the youths traveled about the planet. There were six cities and the underground railway went to each one. They had planned to earn money in their usual way, but discovered the Midwayans had no currency. Everything was free and everybody worked at his job and slept well at night with no worries about repaying interest on loans.

Jesus wanted to bring this perfect society back to Jerusalem, but he could not get the ear of the Lord.

The Problem of Lying About Sex.

Jesus didn't like to stay up late. He preferred self-flagellation and then early to bed. But the Disciples went out every night and made love to the Midwayans. They discovered that half the Midwayans were unisex, so they made love to half of the half that wasn't. The Disciple who understood mathematics calculated that in three thousand years, fifty percent of the Midwayans would probably still carry some traits of their Earth fathers.

When Jesus asked his Disciples where they went at night, they told him they were taking walks, but Jesus suspected they were lying. When I am King of the Jews, he told them, lying about sex will be the most mortal of sins. But the Disciples laughed behind his back. Why, they asked each other, had not the Lord, who was very righteous, included lying about sex in his Ten Commandments, if it was so terrible?

Jesus and the Fig Tree

Jesus was by now desperate to get the Lord's attention. It

came to pass that Jesus craved figs. Spotting a fig tree, he went to see if it had any figs under its leaves, but it wasn't the season for figs and so he found none. Jesus demanded that the tree produce a fig for him, but no fig was forthcoming. Filled with rage, he said to the tree, "You will never bear fruit again." Immediately the tree dried up. Jesus was astonished. Praise the Lord! he exclaimed.

When the Disciples saw what had become of the tree, they were astounded by the power of Jesus. "How did you do that?" they asked. But Jesus never told how he did his magic tricks. He told his Disciples that anyone could dry up a fig tree who was the son of the Lord God Almighty.

But secretly Jesus was disappointed and angry that even after the fig tree miracle, his father remained silent.

The Plague of Insects

Jesus knew that to make his father notice him he would have to do a much greater miracle than dry up one fig tree. He recalled how the Lord had called down a plague of locusts in Egypt to get Pharaoh's attention.

So Jesus worked his magic and conjured up a plague of night insects. In one night they devoured every leaf, tree, and crop on the entire planet. The Midwayans did not have to worry about starving because the insects left behind a miraculous excretion that looked and tasted just like manna.

When God saw what Jesus had done, he was not pleased. Does that whipper-snapper think he can out-plague the Lord? I'll show *him*.

Heavenly Retribution

So the Lord God sent a plague of sand upon the planet. The sand covered the fields and filled in all the natural springs and ponds and lakes. It came right down to the shores of the salt seas. The sand blocked the entrances to the towers, forcing the Midwayans to abandon the buildings by climbing down ropes. Sand got into the subway system and stopped the trains. Even letting in sea water did not wash the sand away.

So that the Midwayans would not all die of thirst, God

created a heavy morning dew. What they did not drink seeped into the ground and fed the plants and grasses deep in the sand so that they could stay alive and grow until the insects attacked them again.

Jesus and the Plague of Stones

When Jesus saw the plague of sand the Lord had wrought, he knew he would have to outdo him. So he conjured up a plague of stones that instantly lay scattered upon the sand all over the planet. The stones prevented anyone ever trying to farm again, but they did provide something to sit on.

After Jesus did this, the Lord said nothing at all and did not respond with a greater plague. Jesus wondered if stones were less impressive than plagues of sand and insects. Perhaps the Lord was laughing at him. Jesus decided he would have to think of a new and better ploy.

The plan Jesus decided on was to kill himself. When he told his Disciples, they were very upset and begged him not to do it. At least not on Midway. "We'll have no way to get home," they told him. But Jesus was unimpressed.

The Suicide Plan

It was clear that Jesus had to come up with a suicide plan quickly if he did not want to be murdered by the Midwayans, who were starting to riot because of the rocks and sand.

He considered climbing one of the abandoned towers and jumping out a window. But he could think of no way to accomplish this without breaking every bone in his body.

Jesus did not really want to kill himself. He just wanted his father to worry about him and be duped into showing his love. So Jesus decided on crucifixion. With the help of his Disciples, he constructed a large cross. They carried the cross up the one hill they had found on the planet. After they had set up the cross, Jesus told them to go away while he worked his magic.

"I swear to you on this cross," he told them as they walked away, "that the next time I come to this planet will not be before three thousand years." Jesus said this because he felt it would take the Midwayans at least that long to forget what had happened and to evolve some food better than manna. To make sure nobody would recognize him, he'd come disguised, and in a space ship.

The Crucifixion

The next day at high noon the Disciples returned to the hill and found Jesus tied to the cross, looking dead. A silence lay upon the land and it appeared that God had forsaken his son. The Disciples worried that even touching Jesus might break his concentration. None of the Midwayans seemed anxious to cut him down either.

That night Jesus climbed down from the cross by himself and rested a few days in a cave.

The Prophesy

While in the cave, Jesus thought long and deep. If ever he hoped to be King of the Jews, he would have to change. If he couldn't fight God, he would have to join him. He would praise the Lord at every opportunity, would out-grovel David-the-Toady, and make any kind of wild promise – paradise, hell, anything. He was determined that even if it took 1000 years, he would be reborn King of the Jews.

Then let his father try and forsake him on the cross!

Soon We Will Return to Jerusalem.

Today Jesus will levitate us back to earth. God has not been completely silent. Last evening two Angels told Jesus that his father sends his regrets and will get back to him. Right now the Lord is busy helping David capture Jerusalem. After that he will make David King of Israel and Judah, and make his descendants kings for ever.

THE EPILOGUE

Next morning, when the Krohs awoke
and looked out at their land,
they saw a most amazing sight.
It all was green,
and not a drop of dew or trace of white
was to be seen on sand or rock.

Then one, who recently was known as Ken,
tried chewing on a tiny shoot,
then snapped it off above the root
and swallowed it right down.
Ken felt the joy of this success
as if he'd reached a terrible divide
and had already crossed it.
But suddenly, in great distress,
his stomach lost it.

And when Ken looked around
and saw upon the Krohtian plain
a thousand others eating grass
who also quickly tossed it,
and then got word through shrug and sigh
it was the same all over Kroh,
he said, I think that we will die.
Could this be God's revenge on us
for having told that lie?

What lie? said one who formerly was Rex.

Well, Rex, said Ken, the other week,
while boning up on Earthspeak,
badminton, croquet,
and every other discipline
we felt was needed to receive
those Earthlings in a cordial way,
I opened up an ancient text

and read therein
that lying about sex is sin.
And Rex, we lied that time
we told the Earthlings
every Kroh was unisex,
although we knew that half were not.

Now wait, said Rex, you're talking rot.
My sole intention was to make
our philosophic argument air tight,
and maybe spare our females
from rude sexual advances.
But hey, you could be right;
I could have told the truth
and let the ladies take their chances.

But then Rex paused, and gave a sigh.
You know, he said, until today
I read those scriptures with a wink of eye,
and blamed our desert landscape
on a meteor from space.
But now that everything we eat we vomit,
and there have been no sightings of a comet,
I think those texts may not be all
preposterous distortions.
To lose our food and drink in one fell swoop
is tragedy of Biblical proportions.

Just then a starving germ came by
and looked the Mentians in the eye.
Said Rex, That germ's about to die.
And die it did, right at their feet.

Said he, who once was known as Moe,
I wonder what germs eat.
Perhaps they need the manna too
and cannot live without their dew.

At this Ken smiled, and said, My friend,
you shouldn't fear we've reached the end.
For in the worst scenario,
if we do die and go to rest beneath the sand,
our flesh and bones will fertilize this land,
and in a dozen centuries
there will again be trees,
and fruit and grain,
and slender towers in the rain,
and maybe even snow.
Does that make you feel better, Moe?

I guess it does, but even so,
if Rabbi Schwister comes back soon,
with invitations for all Krohtians
having Jewish derivations
to emigrate that very afternoon,
I'd really like to go, said Moe.

ABOUT THE AUTHOR

Nina Galen has published novels and articles in the U.S., England and France. The novellas *CROC* and *KROH* are her first written in 'heroic or epic doggerel'.

Galen's novels include *The Rennläufer:* E.P. Dutton; Victor Gollancz (England); Editions Planète (France) *The Grapevine:* Victor Gollancz; Sphere (England) *Monopoly on Terror* (pen name Bruce Buck): Zebra Books, and *Eden Motel* and *To Love Flaminio:* East Palace. She has been published in *Ellery Queen's Mystery Magazine,* and in the scholarly journal, *Nineteenth Century Fiction.* Her aviation articles have appeared in *Flying, Flying's Guide to Instrument Flying,* and *Air Progress,* as well as aviation magazines in England and France.

The author's Commentaries and Features have been produced on Public Radio.

A Special Collection of Galen's publications, manuscripts and personal papers can be found at the CSWR, General Library, University of New Mexico at Albuquerque. There is also a Special Collection of her publications at UCLA.